Being There

The Healing Power of Presence

Michael Forster

kevin mayhew

kevin mayhew

First published in Great Britain in 2015 by Kevin Mayhew Ltd
Buxhall, Stowmarket, Suffolk IP14 3BW
Tel: +44 (0) 1449 737978 Fax: +44 (0) 1449 737834
E-mail: info@kevinmayhew.com

www.kevinmayhew.com

The publishers wish to thank all those who have given their permission to
reproduce copyright material in this publication.

Every effort has been made to trace the owners of copyright material and
we hope that no copyright has been infringed. Pardon is sought and apology
made if the contrary be the case, and a correction will be made in any
reprint of this book.

9 8 7 6 5 4 3 2 1 0

ISBN 978 1 84867 790 6
Catalogue No. 1501486

Cover design by Rob Mortonson
© Image used under licence from Shutterstock Inc.
Edited by Nicki Copeland
Typeset by Angela Selfe

Printed and bound in Great Britain

This book is dedicated to
Revd Brian Tucker
with eternal gratitude for the
healing power of his presence

The background to this book

This book draws together four decades of experience in people-centred work: in teaching, church-based ministry and full-time mental health chaplaincy. During his time as a chaplain, the author successfully undertook a Post-graduate Diploma in Counselling and Psychotherapy at Nottingham Trent University, during the course of which he was able to reflect on the earlier experiences of teaching and ministry in the light of new training and insights.

The reflective process continued against the background of chaplaincy and counselling and this book, written following retirement in 2011, is the outcome.

The names and other identifying details of all clients and colleagues mentioned in this book have been changed to protect their privacy and all the relevant authorities have read and are satisfied that there are no confidentiality issues in the text.

Contents

Acknowledgements

The truth that 'No man is an island' has come home to me repeatedly in the writing of this book – which I now recognise has been a lifetime in development. As well as the publishing professionals whose names appear in the titles, I owe a huge debt to a multitude of people. In particular:

- My parents Revd Eric and Cicely Forster who created a home characterised by love, compassion and respect and in whose presence innumerable others found healing – all of which undoubtedly shaped my concept of pastoral companionship from an early age.

- Revd Bruce Keeble, Head of Pastoral Studies at Regent's Park College, Oxford, during my studies there, and valued personal friend ever since.

- The countless people who, as friends, family, colleagues or 'clients', have been vital to my learning journey and some of whose stories appear in this book.

- Those who have undertaken the specific role of 'critical friends' in reading and helping me to clarify the text: Dave Anderson, Jo Harding, Beryl Johnson, Sally Martin, Nicky Mawer, Antony Sheehan, and – saving the best for last – my wife and critical best friend, Jean Forster.

- Finally: clinical and other staff in the NHS, my valued colleagues and mentors of all religious faiths and of none, who understood that spirituality is not an alternative (or competing) therapy but a quality that pervades all we do together.

Foreword

Healing is vividly and deeply connected to the Christian tradition. So much of the Bible is concerned with helping those with disease and sickness. For too long, however, healing as a ministry has been neglected, forgotten – an artefact of history.

I first met the Reverend Michael Forster in the early summer of 2007: he was my colleague and ultimately he was to become my friend. I had just been named Chief Executive of the NHS Trust where Michael had worked (for a number of years) as a senior chaplain.

Colleague, Chaplain, Friend – that's Michael . . . but when I first spoke to him I instantly recognised that he was something much more: Michael was my *litmus test*. He was someone who knew the difference between right and wrong; someone I could look to as a standard bearer of decency. He had seen good as well as bad times in the NHS, leadership of varying quality and, over time, a loss of focus on the spiritual aspect of the organisation's life.

I can't imagine why he would have looked at me as anything more than the latest in line, the architect of the newest cost improvement programme, the next CEO. I'm sure he had the chance to deploy all his skills in treating me *as if* . . . as if I was worthy even though I was merely the most recent bureaucrat in the fold!

For me, though, Michael was someone whose deep commitment to social justice shone through: he stood for those whose voices were weakened or unheard. He was connected to staff and patients in a way that really caught my attention. He cared, and it showed. Michael really got it . . . that is, he got the fact that healing was more than just technical and physical labour. Michael knew healing took emotional labour.

Being There is a powerful articulation of what compassionate and spiritual relationships can achieve. Michael captures the reader with a narrative born of more than four decades of experience in pastoral care and teaching. No lectures here, though; just deep insights into what it takes to be *present* and to do the emotional labour of healing. There is some theory, of course, but theory rooted in practical experience. Michael has lived it.

This book takes the reader on a veritable road trip from the *unconditional positive regard* of Carl Rogers to the *wounded healer* of Carl Jung. Via Old and New Testament we go – concepts of presence, companionship, truth and trust are our travelling companions. At one point Michael quotes from Martin Luther King's mountain-top speech delivered at the headquarters of The Church Of God in Christ in Memphis, Tennessee. It was the eve of King's assassination. He came to Memphis to be *present* with sanitation workers whose voices were weakened and unheard. In that same speech, Dr King talks about his own road trip on *The Road to Jericho*. He described it as a difficult – indeed, somewhat dangerous – road, and yet he travelled along it anyway.

In a similar way, Michael Forster has travelled a sometimes difficult road, one where he has supported people in profound distress along the way. This has been a journey that has required him to integrate the very best of his spiritual and counselling skills. It is a road trip from which he has learned so much, and the lessons he now generously shares with us.

In a strange twist of fate, I now find myself working in Memphis, Tennessee in a faith-based healthcare organisation called The Church Health Center. We are based just minutes away from The Lorraine Motel, the place where Dr King was gunned down.

Our focus is the *least of these*. There is no litmus test for those who wish to either use or work in our organisation, but we do believe that mind, body and spirit are connected, and this is reflected in how we care. This book will encourage and inform anyone interested in such a connection. They will feel more competent and inspired after reading it. They will understand that healing is a process which makes us whole.

In his book *The Inner Voice of Love* Henri Nouwen writes:

> When suddenly you seem to lose all you thought you had gained, do not despair. Your healing is not a straight line. You must expect setbacks and regressions. Don't say to yourself 'All is lost. I have to start all over again.' This is not true. What you have gained, you have gained.[1]

I imagine the many people Michael Forster has helped along his road trip. I imagine how he has reminded people that they have not lost everything that they have previously gained. In *Being There*, we in turn gain from Michael as he gives us his account of health and healing, of skills and emotional connection, of spirituality and humanity.

Thank you, Michael, my colleague, my chaplain and my friend.

Professor Antony Sheehan,
President of the Church Health Center,
Memphis, Tennessee

---

1   Nouwen, Henri J. M., *The Inner Voice of Love*, (Darton, Longman and Todd 2014).

About the author

Michael Forster grew up in an Anglican vicarage, trained for the Baptist ministry at Regent's Park College, Oxford, and later transferred to the United Reformed Church. He has served a variety of churches as minister, and as a whole-time chaplain in a mental health and learning disability NHS Trust. During his training, Michael became attracted to the work of the psychologist Carl Rogers and later gained a post-graduate diploma in counselling and psychotherapy. Michael is perhaps best known in the churches as a writer of hymns and other worship material. Now retired, his main activities are writing and cabinetmaking. The rest of his time he is busy doing nothing – a duty sadly neglected for far too long.

Author's preface

The scope of the book

When I began discussing this book with the publisher, I found it very difficult to identify the intended readership. Would it be for counsellors and psychotherapists? For ministers in training? For mental health professionals? What about other people with pastoral dimensions to their lives: teachers, social workers, police – parents even? At first I found myself saying, 'All of the above – and also . . .'

I continue to believe that the subject matter and contents are very widely applicable, but for the sake of clarity I have chosen to focus upon ministers and pastoral workers in Christian faith communities.

Having established that, simply to allow the book to be focused rather than unnecessarily diffuse, I believe this book – including the section on spirituality – would be of value to people in a very wide variety of contexts. That is not a comment on the quality of this book but upon the universal nature of spirituality.

Because of the primary focus it is right that I should include a substantial section relating Christian spirituality to the counselling and psychological insights. However, I am deeply convinced that those connections are illuminating also for people who do not view them through the lens of traditional Christian belief but are open on a different level to the wisdom and insights they still find there. For that reason I have approached people whose faith positions are markedly different, and they have kindly read and commented upon the text with a view to ensuring that it communicates well across those boundaries.

We could say, then, that this book is in a very general sense of potential relevance to anyone who is involved in any kind of relationship with another person – which hopefully will be most or all of us. If it is true that simply by being with another person we affect their well-being, then clearly that would apply in all our day-to-day interactions, and not just in a specialised counselling or 'pastoral care' environment.

Because of its applicability in the areas of structured pastoral work and counselling, it will be necessary to address some matters of personal and professional safety, such as supervision, confidentiality and others. However, while it is important to recognise these concerns, they are not subjects that can be treated comprehensively here. People engaged in the sensitive areas of professional or voluntary work should be advised and trained appropriately within their setting. I shall return to this in the final chapter.

Terminology

What are we to each other?

Any discussion of helping relationships raises this issue: how is each party in the relationship to be distinguished for the purpose of clarity? Counsellors – at least in the UK – no longer generally call their clients 'patients'. It is clearly important to make distinctions as the roles, needs and indeed vulnerabilities of both participants are different, but it is very easy for any term we use to become festooned with unhelpful associations around status and power that may then feed back quite unconsciously into the relationship.

For the purposes of this book, the terms 'counsellor' and 'client' generally seem inappropriate, but it is difficult to find terminology that does not present problems. 'Helper' and 'helpee' are sometimes used, but these terms are too open to patronising associations as well as giving the impression of a one-way process wherein one person is helpless and needy while the other is the beneficent satisfier of those needs. This is not only an unhealthy but also a simplistic and inaccurate view.

I have come to view the relationship as, to use a sadly hackneyed but nonetheless appropriate metaphor, a journey, and to see my role as a companion accompanying another on the journey that is theirs to make. We shall clarify this further as we progress, but I can think of no less imperfect approach than to describe the pastoral carer as 'companion'. The person whose journey it is, I have chosen to call the 'other' as I am passionately convinced that recognition and respect for the 'otherness' of the person I am accompanying is fundamental to the relationship. As William C. Placher expresses it: 'I can be in true relation only if I respect the otherness of the other.'[2]

This terminology is, of course, itself not free of negative associations, nor could it be if only because of the fluid nature of language – but in order to continue we need to find some kind of terminology, and these words, I believe, have more positive than negative connotations. So I propose to use them in referring to general matters of pastoral care. I shall, though, revert to the more traditional 'counsellor' or 'chaplain' and 'client' when reflecting on my work in the clinical area where those designations are appropriate.

Like 'carer', the term 'pastoral care' also feels uncomfortable, for generally similar reasons. As I am choosing to refer to the pastoral 'carer' as a companion, it seems not inappropriate to describe the activity itself as 'pastoral companionship'. It might be objected, with some justification, that this is too passive a term, evoking

---

2   Placher, William C., *Narratives of a Vulnerable God* (Westminster John Knox Press, Louisville, Kentucky, 1994), p.79.

images of someone simply sitting alongside another – strangers on a train, perhaps – but surely that is not entirely a bad thing if the purpose of this book is to say that 'being there' is in itself potentially transformational.[3] We shall be unpacking quite carefully what 'being there' means as we progress.

The route plan

One of the principles that most shaped my practice when in the teaching profession was, 'Always progress from the known to the unknown.' We learn best when we can link new information to what we know already, rather than trying to construct abstract concepts in the air. Jesus knew this very well, which is why he spoke so often in parables beginning with farming, family or similarly familiar images and invited people to take imaginative steps from there.

That is why I propose to begin on what will be for most of us familiar ground by thinking about companionship and human relationships, before stepping briefly into the world of counselling where I shall use one of the relational, humanistic models to illuminate some insights about human interaction. By the time we reach that point I am confident that the 'signposting' will help the reader readily to understand – even anticipate – the new concepts as they are introduced. Finally, I shall use what has been learned there to shed what might well for many be fresh light upon some familiar biblical stories and faith concepts.

I know, of course, that the opposite ('Bible-based') approach – beginning with the Bible and then making connections into life – will seem more appropriate to many Christian readers, but there are two reasons why I feel it better to work this way. Firstly, I hope that this book will be read by people other than just Christians – the insights and experiences are, I believe, of value whether one comes from any religious tradition or none – and for those who are not Christian, to begin with the Bible would not be to proceed from the known to the unknown. Secondly, for those who are familiar with Judaeo-Christian tradition, these biblical passages are already overlaid with interpretations and, to be candid, assumptions that can sometimes make it difficult initially to see past them and recognise other equally valuable insights.

I hope to take what will for some Christian people be a fresh approach to the Bible here. So my plan is that by the time we reach that section the links will be forming, the signposts will be in place, and what

---

3 I was interested to learn recently that the word 'companion' actually originates from the French *compaignon*, meaning 'one who shares bread with another' – a particularly appropriate image in terms of the Christian faith tradition.

might be new and unfamiliar ideas will be easier to grasp. However, doing so will not mean having to let go of existing interpretations that are important for us – there is generally no conflict between the traditional interpretations of Scripture and what will be offered here. It is not a case of 'either/or', but rather we shall be discovering further, complementary layers of significance in what are already recognised as multilayered writings.

That is the general plan for our journey. We begin by considering some examples of interactions that may be recognisable – or at least easily imaginable – to us all.

1
Being there

Most of us are familiar, to a greater or lesser extent, with the idea of 'being there' for another person. Hopefully we may know and value in our own lives people who are good to have around in troubled times, even though (or maybe precisely because) they don't try to fix things but are simply there with us. For me, and for my wife, the dedicatee of this book is one such person. So I'd like to look at three quick sketches that I think shed light upon this, and we begin with a rabbit, a monkey and a potato.

Talk to the rabbit

A mental health service user, temporarily living as a resident in a therapeutic community, was attending a review with his consultant psychiatrist along with his named nurse.

'So,' the consultant observed, 'I gather you've been managing your anger much better these days.'

'Oh, yes,' replied the patient. 'That's all down to Edgar – he's been really helpful.'

'Would you like to tell me more?'

'Well, he's great, is Edgar – he's always there for me. And whenever I feel angry, instead of lashing out, I go and talk to Edgar for a bit. I always feel a lot better afterwards, and talking it through helps me see it differently and find other ways of handling it.'

The consultant was glancing down the list of staff involved in the patient's care. 'That's really good news! I'm just wondering who Edgar is – I don't see anyone of that name down here. Is he a relative or friend, perhaps?'

Embarrassed, the named nurse shuffled in her seat and looked at her shoes as she said, 'Well, actually . . . Edgar's the unit's pet rabbit.'

It isn't really that hard to understand what was happening here. Edgar the rabbit had a great asset as a therapist: he didn't talk. He had two large ears, one very small mouth that was usually preoccupied with food processing, and the one never got in the way of the others. Edgar just sat and 'listened'. He could not pass an opinion, could not offer gratuitous advice, and – perhaps most importantly of all – could not judge. The residents in the unit found that particularly helpful, They would climb into the rabbit pen to squat down beside Edgar – often equipped with a few titbits to hold his attention – and start to voice their feelings. As they talked, they began to hear themselves in new ways and were able to process not only their emotions but also the issues that were driving them. It was not surprising that many of them left Edgar's run with a much clearer view on their lives and their problems while Edgar awaited his next client, completely unaware that he was an essential contributor to a highly effective therapeutic process.

Many pastoral companions will have had the experience of being effusively thanked for helping someone to clarify their thoughts, when, in fact, all they have done is provide a focus for the other's thinking aloud. It is, of course, easier for a rabbit to do that than a human being, the latter having to resist the temptation to butt in – and that is without doubt the first discipline that any aspiring pastoral companion must learn.

Watch the monkey

What is it that helps? It's a good question, and one that preoccupies people whose role is to care, whether they be ministers, counsellors or pastoral companions. Much time and money is spent on research trying to answer this question – and it often tends to be rather inconclusive. That's partly because we can't remove from the equation the biggest variable of all – the person of the companion – so we don't really know for sure how far it is a specific approach or school of thought that is benefiting the other and to what extent it is the personality of the individual companion. However, it seems not unlikely (at the very least) that the approach and manner of the companion – and the quality of relationship with the other – might well be the single most important factors.

I am convinced that we can gain some valuable insights from rehabilitation work being done with traumatised animals. Clearly, the distinctions between competing approaches to 'talking therapies' hardly come into play when one is trying to rehabilitate a primate, and the only tools we have are those of environment and relationship. So in this context we are able to see clearly the effects of those two factors without the waters being muddied by competing theoretical models. And what we see is a remarkable illustration of the effect that environment and relationship have on well-being.

I have been particularly struck by the evident success at Dorset's famous ape sanctuary, Monkey World, in working with primates damaged by lifetimes of abuse, whether as tourist attractions, household pets or in experimentation in the drugs and cosmetics industries. Their work has been followed in several series of TV documentary programmes where the progress of individual animals and the social groups in which they live can be observed over significant periods of time. Usually, when they are rescued, the animals are far too damaged ever to hope to return to the wild, so the aim is to enable them to live as natural a life as possible in captivity. To that end, they are introduced to an environment as close to their natural habitat as is realistic, to live in social groups with sensitive monitoring by the keepers and good healthcare from specialist vets.

What strikes me about this is how rapidly the animals begin to change positively. Some even need to learn the basic fact that they are apes and not humans, and how to behave in a social environment that they have never before experienced. Some of the psychological scars clearly remain in evidence and – like physical scars – will probably never fade completely; but the healing is nonetheless real, and positive benefits rapidly begin to show as the apes grow in confidence, learn to socialise and soon display the signs of becoming better-adjusted primates, relatively happy and at ease in their new lives. The significant point is that their healing comes not from the input of a wise minister or counsellor but from exposure to a healthy environment and the opportunity to build (in terms of their own species) normal, healthy social relationships.

There is, of course, an obvious flaw in this comparison: for better or for worse, we are not in a position to rescue and transplant in quite the same way those to whom we are pastoral companions.[4] One of the frustrations many pastors and therapists alike experience is the knowledge that after an hour with us, people will return to the often-unhelpful environments of their daily routines. However, the purpose of observing this work is not that we might construct some kind of template for our helping relationships with people, but rather that it does show – with, I think, quite stark clarity – the importance of a healthy environment, which for our purposes means a psychological one (there is usually little we can do about the physical circumstances).

There is at least one more important thing we learn from observing the work with primates. And the best illustration of that is found if we take a further step away from the world of human interaction and eliminate the sentient element altogether.

---

4 This term will be used throughout the book in place of the more familiar 'carer', as discussed under 'Terminology' in the Author's preface.

Consider the potato

The psychologist Carl Rogers, founder of the school of thought that became the person-centred approach to counselling (on which more later), found inspiration in, of all things, a potato[5] – rather a sad specimen, in fact, left in a cellar without soil or other source of nutrients. What Rogers noticed was that the potato continued to 'try' to grow (something we may all have observed in potatoes left too long in the vegetable rack). From this, he formulated the theory that all living organisms have a natural drive for self-actualisation and development that is active throughout life and cannot be stopped even by a poor environment. More important than that, though, was that the potato, deprived of the necessities for healthy development, grew in unhealthy ways and became distorted, unattractive and probably inedible in the process.

This, he said, happens with all living organisms, including human ones. Put us in a poor environment and our inner drive towards growth and actualisation will continue – but in such an environment, that unstoppable process will be subverted into *unhealthy* development. This is a point I used to make when in healthcare chaplaincy: if we concentrate solely upon a person's clinical need to the neglect of other aspects of their being (in particular for us, their psycho-spiritual needs), then they will not simply put those matters on hold but are likely to be damaged by the continuing drive towards growth.

We are also learning (far too slowly, I fear) that the human organism is a unified whole and a person's mental and spiritual well-being will affect their ability to heal physically. If, for example, someone is ill with appendicitis, then a less holistic approach might suggest that the important thing is the care related to that – medication, surgery, after-care, infection control and so on – while other matters about their human need for warmth, their spirituality, relationships, self-esteem, etc. can all be simply put on hold while the experts concentrate on the job in hand. However, it is now becoming increasingly recognised that if those other matters are well catered for, the patient is likely to recover more quickly and remain well for longer after discharge. Indeed, the value of Pets As Therapy, where appropriately selected animals (e.g. 'PAT dogs') are taken to the ward for patients to stroke, is gaining recognition.

We shall look at this in more depth later, but it is easy to see how it relates to the experience of the monkey sanctuary where animals come in profoundly damaged and – simply by their intelligent introduction

---

5   Rogers, Carl R., *The Foundations of the Person-Centred Approach* (1979). Available at http://www.elementsuk.com/libraryofarticles/foundations.pdf (accessed 19 March 2015).

to a healthy psychological environment – are enabled to become more truly themselves. In Carl Rogers' terms, they progress towards being 'fully functioning'.

So far, we have seen at least three important things which can be summarised by back-tracking along our diversionary route to where we began.

The potato shows us the importance of environment, for good or ill. If Rogers is right (and the evidence seems very compelling that he is), then we cannot help but be affected by our (psychological as well as physical) environment. We cannot stop the internal drive towards growth and development which in a good environment will tend to be healthy, and in a poor one will be to some extent or other maladaptive.

However, from the example of the work among monkeys, we see a vital corollary to that: the possibility of redemption. The work at Monkey World and other similar sanctuaries provides abundant cause to hope that, in sentient beings, at least some of the maladjustment can be reversed and some degree of healing experienced.

And finally, returning us to our point of departure, the rabbit assures us that our simple, wordless presence can have astonishing healing power in the creation of such a helpful and healing environment.

Risky business

One of the things any observer of a primate sanctuary quickly realises is that this process involves accepting and managing risk. The apes are not kept in protective isolation – there would be nothing enabling about that – but are expected to live in social groups that resemble as closely as practicable the situation that would apply in the wild. The adaptation process can be scary and downright dangerous as they learn, for example, how to find their appropriate place within the hierarchical structure and build their own social relationships within those constraints. The keepers' role in this is apparently to observe and provide support, intervening when appropriate but also knowing when to stand back and allow conflicts to be resolved by the apes themselves. Rather than protecting the animals, the staff are there to enable them to cope with the day-to-day problems and conflicts – and to experience the joys and fulfilments – of life in their own society.

This highlights one of the basic dilemmas of human relationships: when should we intervene directly to protect, help or advise the people whose companions we are, and when would doing that simply create dependence, stunt personal growth or change our relationship in other detrimental ways? Again, we can see from the backstories of the rescued and rehabilitated primates how our well-intentioned attempts to 'care' for another (assuming, of course, that we have the range of skills required to do so) can make it impossible for someone to function in their social environment – and how that can be transformed by a more creative risk-acceptant approach. Every parent, every teacher and youth worker – indeed, every one of us in some part of our lives – has to make judgements about that. Sometimes – hopefully more often than not – we get them right, but sometimes we don't, and any seasoned pastoral companion must almost certainly have had to learn from that experience at some time.

What all of this is amounting to is that what has traditionally been called 'pastoral care' is much less about 'caring for' someone in a quasi-clinical sense, and much more about providing a psychological environment where they can find and come to trust their own resources for becoming.

The resident in the therapeutic community whom we met at the beginning of this chapter was not suffering from delusions and, of course, knew perfectly well that Edgar was not literally listening – still less, talking – to him. Edgar provided a focus and, if you like, gave him permission to speak when no one else was going to interfere, and in doing so helped him to discover his own inner resources. He became more confident that much of the help he needed was 'in here' rather than 'out there', and came to trust his own considered judgements.

Therein, though, lies an important difference that we have to recognise. The resident knew that if Edgar wandered off or turned away, it was not a personal slight against him – and it did not affect the value of the session. In the case of a human presence, however, things are obviously very different in this regard. A therapist who requires a constant supply of food in order to hold their attention, and whose gaze occasionally shifts to look at the scenery outside, would not be tolerated in the same way.

So it is now time to consider what it is about the presence of another *person* that is helpful.

2
Qualities of presence

'To look the other honestly in the face is to encounter someone I cannot control.'[6]

Reading those words for the first time set off a mental firework show, with light exploding all around me, illuminating my world in new ways. In truth, though, the light did not so much reveal new things as show my existing landscape in a sharper relief and a different light. Important aspects of my principles and practice showed up with renewed clarity in the light of this quite simple truth: the more honestly I can look the other in the face (the more I can recognise and respect their 'otherness'), the more powerful my presence is likely to be.

This is the bedrock of pastoral companionship, whichever of its myriad forms it may take. Probably the most widespread of those forms is the simple act of visiting someone with no other purpose than to maintain friendship or keep them company. The value of this cannot be overstated: countless people give their time simply to go and drink tea in another's home or perhaps meet for a walk in the park. They might be surprised to know that they are involved in 'pastoral work', but the value of it becomes much more apparent when we consider the growing awareness of loneliness in our society and the effect that it has. If all this book does is affirm the infinite value of this simplest form of 'being with', and encourage more people to do it, then the time spent writing will have been worthwhile. In all the other things we shall need to consider, we should never lose sight of the power and importance of this simple presence. It may be – and often is – the case that no more than this is needed; but sometimes just this kind of presence can reveal the need for – and open the way to – life-changing processes of healing.

I encountered during my ministry a lady who had come to regard herself as 'born to be abused' – simply there for anyone and everyone to make use of in whatever way they chose. After one of the fairly lengthy silences that characterised our sessions, she looked at me steadily for a few moments and said, 'You don't want anything from me, do you?'

The quiet matter-of-fact tone belied the mind-blowing significance of the moment. For someone who had never before been 'other' but

---

6   Placher, *Narratives of a Vulnerable God*, p.70.

always an extension of other people's 'my', this was a profound – and as it turned out life-changing – realisation. It was, on some levels, similarly profound for her minister. All the long, unspeakably difficult silences, the all-too-frequent sessions where it had seemed that 'nothing' was happening, had all been part of a process by which she reached this pivotal insight. And the key to it all had been my simply being there, allowing her to believe in the previously unthinkable: that she could relate to another human being without fear of exploitation; that she had value and worth and was able to experience genuine respect. That session was to be a key learning experience for me in terms of trusting the process – and the healing power of presence.

However, we do not need to be working with seriously traumatised people for this value to be appreciated.

I found myself reflecting on my earlier careers, thinking of the 'others' I had been unable to control and who – once I accepted that – had taught me so much about relationships.

I remembered pupils with serious musical talent and potential who didn't pursue the careers that I had hoped (and one or two whose talent I had clearly underrated who later surprised me). I remembered under-performing students whose over-controlling parents or teachers had to learn the same lesson I did – and who blossomed when given the space they craved. I remembered another, beset by anorexia, who eventually managed to get into her teachers' and youth leaders' heads that she wasn't going to be persuaded to eat by us or anyone else because deep-seated feelings will not be changed through reasoned argument, but who blossomed into new life, marriage and motherhood when she eventually found people who allowed and trusted her to be 'other' – to be herself and not who the world thought she ought to be. That pupil undoubtedly taught me more important things than I ever taught her!

But the daddy of them all – the one who single-handedly and utterly unwittingly revolutionised my approach to teaching – was 'Jeremy'. When it was known among the staff that he was coming to me for clarinet lessons, I was endowed by my colleagues with an aura of sympathy. In the staffroom, Jeremy's very name was a byword for failure and frustration; he was generally held to be not only incapable of the most elementary learning but utterly disinterested to boot. Words like 'lazy', 'apathetic' and 'no-hoper' tripped off his teachers' tongues with chilling ease – and for a while I thought they were right as I struggled to get Jeremy to understand the basic elements of printed music. If he could not do this, how did he ever hope to play in a satisfying way?

His – and my – salvation arrived in the person of another teacher interrupting his lesson for a quick word with me. We stepped out of the room, leaving Jeremy alone, and as we talked I became aware of music coming through the door. It was simple stuff, certainly, but not without charm – and it surely couldn't be being produced by the boy I had left alone in there? As I re-entered, Jeremy looked sheepish and stopped playing – but I wanted to hear more. A few simple experiments established that he had the ability to reproduce simple melodies by ear, without the help of sheet music – indeed, he found the absence of that positively liberating. And as well as that – to judge by what I had heard through the door – he had an embryonic flair for improvisation. In the latter respect, particularly, he was streets ahead of his teacher! What he could not do was get his head around the 'tadpoles on telephone wires' without which I, although a professionally trained musician, was reduced to artistic incoherence!

It only occurred to me later (after further learning experiences) that for all the staffroom derision, Jeremy had much in common with some of the most successful rock and pop musicians of our – or perhaps all – time.

The long summer break was approaching and I seized each day, radically rethinking my approach to teaching beginners and writing my own primer to go with it. From that time on, beginner students of mine would, I was determined, have a very different learning experience. I would not have used these words at the time, but what it amounted to was that, from first meeting, I would look the other honestly in the face and recognise someone I could not control.

And Jeremy? To be honest, my memory fails – and I'm sure that had he become a great player it would not have. My hope for him, though, is that he might have surprised and taught a few of his other teachers as he had me, and that he came to know and love the clever, intuitive, artistic Jeremy that years of unimaginative 'education' had buried under layers of derision.

Importantly, as I look back on four decades of teaching, pastoral work and counselling, I can't think of a single 'other' who did exactly what I privately expected they would or thought they should in terms of the shape and direction of their lives. That's the risk as well as the adventure (can we have the latter without the former?) of helping relationships. However, to the best of my knowledge, they all went on to live full and healthful lives – many of them beyond anything that had seemed possible on first meeting – but did so in ways that I would never have thought to suggest.

This looking the other honestly in the face is surely the starting point for a healing presence. How can we possibly help another to heal if we cannot recognise their selfhood? What other characteristics must such a presence have?

A trusted presence

If we are to offer help to others, then trust is clearly a given requirement. The trust of the other is the most vital and indispensable resource we have, and it is, of course, not something we can carry around with us in our briefcases. Indeed, it is never really ours at all. Trust is something the other places in us and can – will – withdraw at any time if it appears to be misplaced.

As I began the placement that was part of my counselling training, my first client was referred to me. I was told she had already had two abortive attempts at forming a therapeutic alliance with other counsellors. The clear implication was that I had a bit of a hill to climb from the start. At our first meeting, we discussed the 'contract' – not, in the conventions of this agency, a written document, but the shared understanding of how we would work together and what each might expect of the other. The client was clearly still angry about my predecessor who apparently had failed to attend for her session a number of times without informing the client in advance. It should not require much imagination to have a sense of how devaluing that feels to a person who may already have experienced belittlement in other ways and could quite possibly have issues around self-esteem. None of that, of course, should be assumed, but we should be aware of the possibility of it – leaving aside the matter of general respect and good manners.

It would have been easy for me to have trotted out a simple (and if I'm honest, smug) assurance that 'I would certainly never behave in that way'. However, I felt it better to be more realistic in my approach. I said I would never knowingly or deliberately let her down, but there were a couple of things that I would like to be open about as we began. The first was that my 'day job' involved responding to emergencies and other unexpected calls that sometimes could not be put off until later. If such a thing happened then I would do my best to contact her and let her know, as long as the nature of the emergency allowed. I asked her permission to send the message if necessary through a secretary or other trusted colleague (this would clearly involve giving that person her name and telephone number, and they would almost certainly guess the nature of our connection). She agreed with this, and I then went on to the second – and more delicate – point.

To be candid, administration is not the area of life and work in which I have the most glowing record – more honestly, I am terrible at it (and experience tells me I am far from alone among ministers in this respect!) – and while I would never be knowingly neglectful, a mistake might easily happen at some time. To deal with this, I gave her the number of my counselling service mobile phone and invited her to ring that number if ever I were late for an appointment without informing her. I'm glad to say she never had cause to use it, but it did help to get our working relationship off to a good start. She told me that she valued my honesty and would be willing to agree to a few sessions and see how she felt later.

Our work together went on for many months, until a work opportunity caused her to move out of the area – so apparently we did get something right between the two of us!

Sadly, as I learned by experience, it is less unusual than it should be for people to have been in some way let down by those who have tried to help them. There may be all kinds of reasons for this, from extraordinary events that sometimes disrupt the best-regulated of lives, driving out all awareness of whatever it was we were supposed to do next, to the overwhelming realisation that the task is bigger than we took it to be when we rashly said, 'I'll always be here for you, come what may.' For that reason it is always important to be realistic in our promises and honest about our abilities and limitations. 'I'll do my best to be here for you in whatever appropriate ways I'm able,' is a far better way to word a statement of commitment.

Confidentiality

I shall be looking at this in more depth later, in chapter 10 when we consider matters of ethics and good practice, but it has to be mentioned here as perhaps the most vital condition of trust. That is as it should be. Once a trusting relationship is established, people may well tell their counsellor or pastoral companion things that are hidden from the very nearest and dearest of their family and friends. 'Absolute' is not a word I use easily, and I certainly would not use it here, as confidentiality does have necessary limitations which will be considered in the final chapter. For now, though, it is important to recognise that the bar is set very high indeed in terms of the disclosure to others of anything that is said in a session.

Sad though it is, it has to be said that experience has not given me much assurance about the way confidentiality is understood in society generally. This is, of course, a generalisation and there are honourable exceptions, but the popular understanding is clearly dangerously flawed. Far too often, it is considered perfectly right and proper that the companion's life-partner should be told: 'We don't have secrets from one another' is undoubtedly a laudable principle in terms of family values, but not one to extend to the pastoral confidences of third parties.[7] One minister I knew openly admitted that he shared all confidences with his wife 'because biblically we are one'. He appeared to require time to think about my challenge – that if he were taking that biblical passage so literally – and simplistically – then surely he had no need to tell her as she would know anyway! We need to be clear: 'This is confidential' is not the same thing as 'Don't tell anyone other than your partner'.

At the other end of the scale, one of my pastoral tutors at theological college said that his wife was a truly valuable source of confidence in him among his congregation because she always responded to any gossip with a shrug and the wry comment, 'Oh, don't ask me – my husband never tells me anything!' It is not hard to guess which of those two ministers enjoyed more confidence and trust from his congregation.

It is important to be clear that not telling someone something they have no need or right to know is not a sign of lack of trust – which is how it is sometimes perceived: 'But surely you know you can trust me' has been said to me countless times. The question is not about who can be trusted, but about whom the rightful owner of the information decides may have it. Information given to me in confidence is not mine to dispose of as I think fit. It is held in trust on behalf of the person who confided it to me.

We shall look at this in a little more detail when considering safeguards, but it has been important to recognise it here as we consider the essential matter of trust in the pastoral relationship. Here we have considered three components of that trust:

- The companion's dependability in terms of commitment to the other
- The companion's honesty and awareness of their own limitations and realism about what they are able to offer
- The companion's trustworthiness with sensitive personal information.

It may seem a truism, but the last thing a hurting person needs is more unnecessary pain or insecurity. If the journey of recovery is to be made, it is important that the companion is seen as, in every way that matters, a safe pair of hands for whatever is placed in them.

---

7   We shall consider the vital differences between confidentiality and secrecy in the final chapter.

A truthful presence

We have seen the importance of trust between companion and other – something that I actually feel uncomfortable to say as the very act of mentioning it almost seems to undermine just how obvious it should be! Trust is the indispensable condition of any kind of pastoral work and must not be put at risk even for the most laudable of reasons. For that reason, I who am notoriously wary of absolutism am going to use the forbidden word and say that I believe we should absolutely never be untruthful to the people whose companions we are.

At this point I anticipate gasps of horror from many readers: surely I would not approve of lying anyway, under any circumstances – so why even mention it? Of course that's correct – well, almost . . . I don't suppose I'm the only person who, wanting to give someone a surprise birthday party, for example, might have invented some utterly spurious cover story to prevent them from discovering it too soon. One such event – my wife's sixtieth birthday celebration – was actually held at a venue some distance away where a lot of family members live, and for a good 90 minutes in the close confines of our car I had to sustain an elaborate and rapidly thinning fiction about why we were going all that way!

There was, of course, no serious intent to deceive in this instance – the whole comedy of errors was directed to the moment when my wife would learn the truth – and, while she might well experience some suspicion on future car journeys, there would be no undermining of trust between us, which is the crucial point in this discussion.

Returning, then, to the serious subject in hand: why, we might ask, would anyone not tell the truth to someone towards whom they had pastoral responsibility? Firstly, we need to be clear what I am thinking about here – the question, 'What is truth?' was preoccupying better philosophers than Pontius Pilate for centuries before his infamous encounter with Jesus (John 18:38), and still does so now! This is more a matter of what Kate McClelland calls 'honest information giving'[8] about matters of what for brevity we might call 'fact' – not, for example, discussions about another's subjective experiences or my personal beliefs, which are quite another subject that I shall come to shortly.

I was present at a church training event where a number of carers and volunteers were discussing this very issue, which in that instance centred upon the use of the reply 'I don't know' when the other asked for information that the carers and volunteers were not comfortable to give – most usually because it was bad news that they

---

8   McClelland, Kate, *Call the Chaplain* (Canterbury Press 2014).

thought the other would be happier not knowing. They anticipated (often correctly) that if the other knew they had the information, then it would be difficult to justify withholding it and all kinds of difficulties would follow which could, they felt, be circumvented by the simple 'white lie' – hence the reply, 'I don't know.' The trouble is, though, that once the step has been taken of telling direct lies (whatever colour we consider them to be) in our role as companions, the nature of the relationship has changed, most probably for ever.

This does not mean, of course, that any information requested by the other must simply be blurted out! There are ways – not to mention times and places – that are more or less appropriate for the imparting of bad news; and sometimes it may simply not be our place to dispense it even if we know. All of that can be covered in a variety of ways – but pretending not to know the answer is not one of them.

Very early in my ministry, I watched a family endure terrible agonies because of this. A young mother was terminally ill, and it had been decided by well-meaning carers that she would be happier not knowing the prognosis. Sadly, those being less-enlightened days, the care professionals went along with the family's wishes even to the point of giving misleading – and transparently conflicting – information to the patient about the nature of the illness.[9] The result was a serious breakdown of trust and weeks of unspeakable pain for a lovely and loving family who simply did not know how to cope and, instead of being drawn together to share this most intimate and important of all life processes, they found themselves alienated, angry and lonely as individuals within the family home.

Far too inexperienced (and without the support I now know I should have had), I confess I was in over my head by several fathoms. My attempts to persuade the family to allow me to say what they found unsayable were completely ineffectual, and my dread of causing more conflict and pain so inhibited my faithfulness to my own calling that I became bogged down in the situation and as helpless as everyone else. However, for reasons I could not then work out, it later turned out that my being there in that process, for all my feelings of helplessness and ineptitude – and indeed for all my outright failings – had had a value that allowed me to continue to work with the family after the death. But the whole experience left me with painful lessons to learn. I had become caught up in a well-meaning but ill-advised collusion to conceal vital information from the person most entitled to know it – but worse than that, in the

---

9 It should be noted that this would have been considered poor – even unethical –
    practice even then, but was far from uncommon; and even though official policy is
    clear, it remains in practice a painful issue for caring, sensitive nurses and other carers
    now.

equally well-meaning deception that left the other feeling betrayed by everyone including the minister: if she could not expect honesty from me, then from whom?

I came to learn much from this about the positive and negative aspects of presence. My evasiveness and failure to be open with the dying lady undoubtedly compromised the value of my presence with and towards her – although she still seemed to welcome my visits even so. For her family, it seemed that the presence of someone who was apparently willing to inhabit their nightmare with them – and to remain there despite such obvious powerlessness and confusion – had a value that was completely beyond my comprehension at the time. For the remaining years that I stayed in that area, I continued to visit and be warmly welcomed at the family home.

We shall look later at some of this when considering spiritual insights, particularly in chapters 7 and 8 when we reflect on the birth and the dying of Jesus. I can say here, though, that this sad story highlights the importance of supervision and support for pastoral companions as well as ministers. To put it simply, no minister or pastoral companion – even with much more training and experience than I had at the time – should be so isolated, and there is an urgent need for faith communities and denominational councils seriously to address the whole long-overdue issue of support and supervision for pastoral workers, whether paid or voluntary.

For us, here and now, there is more to be said about this whole matter of openness in pastoral relationships.

It may be that the companion or carer is asked for information that they are in truth not the best people to give, or that that particular time or place is inappropriate. All those circumstances can be covered with a simple, truthful explanation of those points: 'The doctor is going to talk to you about that,' or 'This isn't the best time/place for that – but I promise to talk about it with you very soon' – a valid reply, but only if the companion is determined to see that it happens.

Clearly, there are some matters best communicated by people whose role and professional knowledge make them better placed to answer any questions – or it just might be that there is someone who enjoys a particularly high level of trust with the other and would be heard better by them. In a clinical context, both of those were familiar scenarios. I might be asked by a client about anticipated changes in treatment, or by a family member for information about the client that I had not been specifically permitted by them to give. In such cases, most of the participants in the training event I referred to earlier felt it would be appropriate to say, 'I don't know,' but I disagreed then and I have never changed that view. Admittedly, rather than get into an unhelpful and unnecessary confrontation, I might sometimes permit myself a certain evasiveness and use a reply such as, 'I really couldn't say,' in the hope that the person would accept that and make their own assumptions. However, I would never put myself in the position of having to defend an outright lie by explicitly saying, 'I don't know,' where that was not the case. Just one exposure of that single act of mendacity and the possibility of good pastoral work and all the fruit it may produce in the future is at least undermined if not destroyed.

Sometimes the person would see through my evasive answer and say, 'You "can't say" – but you do *know*, though, don't you?!' and at that point I would explain that I did have the information but for whatever reasons was not in a position to disclose it. Usually, I could ease the sense of rejection by referring the other to the appropriate person: 'You need to speak to your partner (GP, social worker, etc.) about that.' Sometimes, if pressed, I might say that it would be unethical for me as a pastoral companion, chaplain or whatever my role might be, to speak about things that were outside my area of expertise.

It may well be that some of the others we work with will find our refusal to disclose available information positively infuriating – but if anything it is likely over time to reinforce rather than undermine trust.

Sometimes, of course, it may be that we have less worthy reasons for trying to withhold information.

A psychotherapist colleague spoke in group supervision about a client who – for a variety of reasons – had a tendency to be prickly and with whom maintaining a respectful relationship could sometimes be a challenge. During a session, a peculiarity in the client's name connected in his mind with aspects of the client's behaviour and caused the therapist involuntarily to smile. Although he quickly suppressed it, he was not in time to prevent the client noticing.

'Why did you smile?'

The thought had been less than complimentary to the client, and the therapist, in a state of embarrassment, tried to deflect the question. The rest of the session became a nightmare of ducking and diving as the therapist attempted unsuccessfully to deflect the client's determined probing. Before their next meeting, the therapist took the incident to his clinical supervisor where the issue could be explored, and his supervisor was very clear: 'You have to tell the truth; you have no choice in the matter.' Clearly, the client was not going to be fobbed off, and effective therapy was out of the question while this issue hung over the sessions. Some convincing reply simply had to be given, and that meant either the truth or a lie. And the supervisor was very clear in confirming what the therapist already knew: he could not lie to his client, which only left one option.

The dreaded hour arrived and the therapist made his confession. To his astonishment and relief, the client saw the joke, roared with laughter and the air was cleared for therapy to continue.

The question might be raised about how the therapist would have dealt with it had the client responded in the way that had been expected. We need not concern ourselves with that, but the relevant point here is that, without the therapist being honest with the client, the therapeutic alliance would have been wrecked in any case.

What is truth?

The question Pilate famously asked Jesus (and which Jesus was wise enough to ignore – or in any case, which the Gospel writer significantly leaves hanging in the air) takes us into a different aspect of openness. Sometimes, what is true for one person is not true for another. This is important to remember when someone says, 'You do believe me, don't you?' Being believed is an important part of being valued, and this question can put a pastoral companion in a quandary, not wanting to add further to the other's distress by saying, 'Frankly, no!' It may be helpful to consider what it is we are asked to believe to be true.

A person may feel demeaned by something that has been said or done, even if it is not actually true that whoever did it intended that. For example, a simple if tactless remark intended to show interest – such as, 'You were wearing that dress last Wednesday' – could easily be taken to be a criticism or a dig. Sometimes people affected by such negative experiences then feel further demeaned by other people's (again often well-meaning) attempts to find other explanations, and 'I'm sure she didn't mean it that way' is mistakenly heard as 'That's not true – I don't believe you.' It is not unusual for a person to seek affirmation in trying to find someone who will believe them, and the pastoral companion's role there is vital. The other is seeking personal affirmation of their selfhood, not to have their feelings of belittlement or whatever they may be confirmed. I can believe that person's truth as their truth – I can believe that *they* experienced being demeaned or insulted; I can believe that someone *experienced* reality very differently from the way I do; I can believe a person who says that they experienced a fantastic event that caused them to feel elated or terrified. I can believe all that even while interpreting the event itself differently.

Often the most helpful thing is to focus on the experience and the feelings it generated without apparently validating it as a shared truth: 'You found those words really hurtful.' Sometimes I would, if pressed to answer directly, reply that I did believe the other's experience but if I'm honest would *interpret* it differently. What I would never do would be to give spurious validation to their interpretation by a simple but mendacious 'Yes'.

The question behind the question

It is very important to develop a sense for what underlies the questions we're asked. Someone who asks whether we believe in heaven may not be particularly interested in a theological discussion but be speaking out of a deep fear that their unexplained symptoms are life threatening.

I remember being asked whether I believe in the devil – a question not uncommon for ministers in all kinds of contexts, and sometimes used as a quick way of establishing whether one's theology is 'sound'. For someone with a bit of a liking for philosophical debate, there is ample material there to tempt me! 'It depends what you mean by . . .' leads into all kinds of fascinating territory about the nature of belief, evil, freedom and so on. However, a little probing behind the question confirmed that this person really did not want any of that but was simply, desperately, seeking some kind of explanation for the catalogue of misfortunes that had unexpectedly come his way. His question was really about why, in the words of Rabbi Harold Kushner, 'bad things happen to good people'.[10] And underlying that, of course, were many other questions about whether he indeed was a good person or something different.

In that instance, a truthful reply to the presenting question would have been distracting at best, and might well have ended up with my struggling to defend my position as a person of faith to another whose mark of 'faith' was very different, rather than addressing his needs. In that case, the session would have turned into being all about me and not about the other. It was important to identify the real question being asked before leaping in with an answer.

The right to remain silent

Openness does not, of course, mean that we are obliged to give direct answers to whatever questions are asked of us. There may be any number of reasons why this is not appropriate. In the instance above, for example, had it turned out to have been the case that I was being tested as to the authenticity of my faith position, then I would almost certainly have declined to answer and explained my reasons. There are within the Christian religion – or any religion, for that matter – many strands of belief and opinion, and there are groupings of believers who take different views about the 'essentials' of faith. For many Christians, those tend to be around the literal acceptance

---

10 Kushner, Harold, *When Bad Things Happen to Good People* (Pan 2002).

of beliefs such as the six-day creation process in Genesis, Mary's virginal conception of Jesus, the bodily resurrection of Jesus from the dead and, of course, the existence or otherwise of the devil, to name but four among many. It's easy to see how quickly a pastoral conversation could be sidetracked into a blind alley, and my role as a minister, chaplain, pastoral companion – or indeed as a teacher in earlier times – was to be there for the benefit of others in whatever ways were appropriate and within my ability. So I would usually do my best to keep the focus on the needs of the other, and not upon my own personal beliefs or circumstances.

There may be many other instances including, for example, personal questions about matters we prefer to keep private. That can cover all kinds of areas. In clinical practice, for example, if people asked where I lived, I would only give the county, not the town or village and certainly not an address or phone number – apart from anything else, chaplains have families whose well-being matters. For a pastoral companion it might just be a matter of not feeling comfortable discussing family matters (we are entitled to have private lives, like anyone else), or a very proper concern to prevent pastoral conversations becoming sidetracked and to keep the focus on the other. Whatever it is, we do not need to be open to the point of transparency in our personal lives – but we do need to be honest about the limits we set.

But you would say that, wouldn't you?!

I was once put on the spot by a very direct, no-nonsense approach from someone seeking support, who asked about my personal beliefs: 'I've got a question for you – but I know what your answer will be so I don't really know why I'm bothering to ask. You're bound to follow the party line because you're paid by the Church.'

That was not actually true – at this point in my career I was entirely paid by the NHS – but I tried to assure him that (while I recognised the general reality of his premise) I personally have never found party lines easy to swallow, with or without the hook and sinker. He then went on to ask about whether I personally believed, in the most literal sense, a particular example of Christian doctrine – finishing with a repeat of his statement that I was bound to say what my Church expected me to believe rather than be honest.

Exploration of his reasons for asking the question assured me that this was a genuine case of someone struggling with the tension between what he felt he was expected to believe and some undermining questions that he felt were reasonable to ask and would not go away just for being ignored. So, having established as far as I could that a conversation about theology was the appropriate response, I began by discussing with him the different ways in which things can be read – and in particular the point that religious experience is often by definition beyond the capacity of language to capture, so that people will use the most descriptive and vivid images and metaphors that come closest to their experiences. It is not, then, necessarily a mark of someone's faith that those things are taken literally.

Well, I had tried – but I was not to be allowed off the hook so easily, and the other took my apparent vacillation to indicate that I did not feel able to answer honestly. There was not (as might conceivably have been the case) any clinical or therapeutic reason not to answer the question, so I stated with complete candour that I interpreted the doctrine in question as expressing a mysterious reality that could only be described in that way. Did I believe that the original experience was exactly as described? Clearly not – but that did not mean that it was not 'real'. Our conversation took a philosophical turn as we discussed the relationship between 'truth' and 'fact', and I have to admit it was very enjoyable!

We met a number of times after that; whenever he had a spell as an in-patient he would ask to see me, and always referred to me as 'the chaplain who tells the truth'. I often told him that I would confidently hope that under these circumstances any of my colleagues would have been similarly open.

The key point for him was that our first encounter so assured him that he could trust me that he was able to say things that otherwise would have been impossible for him – and that in turn enhanced the effectiveness of our sessions.

This encounter tells us much about the hill that religious functionaries may have to climb in order to be taken seriously and trusted. This gentleman was by no means alone in his distrust not only of clergy but also of representatives of any institution.

I have considered here a number of aspects of truth-telling in the context of our responsibility not to be deliberately dishonest with others, and have suggested that there are a number of facets to this. It should not be thought, however, that this is an area for clever, legalistic semantics or double-talk. Certainly, we should do our best to identify just what truth it is that is being asked for, and then consider whether it is within our remit to give it. Having done that, we must be honest with others, even if that ultimately means saying, 'I do have that information but for reasons of x or y I am not able to tell it to you.' As I indicated earlier, this is one of the few areas of life where I use the language of absolutism. If we are to have relationships of trust with the others whose journeys we are privileged to share as companions, then it must be because we are trustworthy – and not that we are making a convincing pretence at it, however honourably motivated. The difficulties that that raises for us are for us to deal with – and if we want the privilege of being companions, then that is the cost we accept.

An active presence

'Being present to' another is not the same as simply being in the room – although sometimes that is enough, and we need to be aware when it is and not over-egg the pudding with words and actions. The skill is in sensing when to keep silent and when (and how) to speak. But is there not something strange – even incongruous – about this heading? One of the main points that I am making in this book is that we should trust the power of simply being there and resist the urge to intervene inappropriately in the lives of the others whose journey we share – so why, one might well ask, introduce the subject of being 'active'?

It is not as inappropriate as it might seem. The essential distinction is between, on the one hand, appropriate 'activity' that makes our presence with the other more effective ('actively being with') and, on the other, actions that we might undertake either on behalf of the other (such as functioning as an advocate or representative) or with a view to persuading or changing the other in some way. It is the former kind of activity that is our subject here.

In reflecting upon the effectiveness of the rabbit as a presence, I observed that the patients concerned would have expected – did indeed expect – rather more from their human companions. Edgar would not know better than to turn away or lollop to the other side of his pen if the impulse took him, and this his 'clients' knew and accepted – but when they were speaking with nurses, doctors or indeed chaplains, they did expect something just a little more attentive than that!

Listening skills

Listening is an activity – one that has a power we must never underestimate. It seems to be a universal human experience that being respectfully listened to – being heard and understood – is profoundly affirming. What we clearly need to do, for that to be best experienced, is to find ways not only of hearing people clearly but of *showing* that we listen, that we care, that the story is important to us, without interrupting or steering the flow (and without ostentatiously making a show of it). There are various ways we can do this – and they can also help to facilitate the flow when needed. Let's take first things first.

Eye contact

I am reminded of visits to my excellent local GP. In my mind's eye, I see him turning his swivel chair so that his whole body is angled less towards his desktop computer and more towards me – a deeply symbolic as well as pragmatic act. He does not crowd in on me in a confrontational way but makes enough movement for it to be clear where his attention lies. I can never help but be reminded – by way of contrast – of another GP from years ago who quite unwittingly made me feel very differently as he kept his gaze firmly fixed on his computer and fired questions at me while typing. It took me a while to recognise that he was not 'multi-tasking' but actually referring to my notes on his screen as he listened, and typing in my responses contemporaneously to ensure accuracy. I have no doubt that he was doing all this with the highest of good intentions in order to ensure that from a clinical point of view he offered the best care – but to me it just felt alienating and devaluing. There would, of course, have been ways open to him to combine the best of both approaches as my current GP does, by the use of simple verbal conventions such as, 'Excuse me while I just look that up in your notes,' and so on.

I recall a comment about such practice by my line manager during my early years in chaplaincy: 'Our clients do not have a right to expect that we will perfectly remember every little thing they say – but they do have a right to have our full attention when they are speaking to us!'

It's important to maintain eye contact in a sensitive way so that it does not degenerate into a blank stare or come to feel threatening to the other. Over time, I learned some approaches that were helpful to particular people, by which I would shift my gaze slightly when I detected that it was appropriate and then return after a few seconds, making it clear by one of a number of devices that I had been listening in that time. Not that I always got it right by any means . . .

An occasion comes to mind when I was severely taken to task by a very angry gentleman who aggressively complained about my 'sullen face'. I was astounded, as the last thing I felt was sullen. I was attempting to maintain eye contact while avoiding registering either disapproval or approval of his words because I did not want to influence his willingness to say things to me. Evidently I had allowed my face to become fixed, which he then interpreted as a negative response. It was a very important lesson for me to learn.

Having said that, in most cases there is more likely to be an issue with lack of eye contact than with an excess of it. It is important to be particularly careful not to shift one's gaze at a moment that could (however mistakenly) appear to the other to be loaded. If someone is disclosing something that they might think controversial, then for their companion to seem to be avoiding their eyes would not usually be helpful. If the other should avert their gaze, generally speaking, it's important that when they return they find the companion still attentive to them. Simple movements like nodding encouragingly as a story unfolds can be helpful – as long as the nodding does not appear to be impatiently saying, 'I know, I know,' or 'Get on with it'! In all these areas it is a matter for good sense, sensitivity and awareness that can only come through experience.

Non-verbal responses

As already mentioned, simple movements and changes of expression can be useful – just something to show the other that their words are being attended to. Sometimes a change of body position may be helpful. Many people will have heard of 'mirroring', where two people engaged in conversation find themselves adopting similar postures. This can be a non-verbal indication of attentiveness and empathy – although it can also look contrived and even mocking (especially if the other has some marked unusual habits in this area). Personally, I have never consciously mirrored another during a pastoral session, but have sometimes become aware of it after it has happened.

The important thing is simply to find ways of ensuring that the other knows we are valuing them and giving them our attention, without unnecessarily interrupting the flow.

Minimal encouragers

It is quite a simple matter to encourage the flow without interrupting it – and most of us do it without thinking in general conversation. Those little sounds we utter: 'Mm-hmm', 'uh-huh', and so on, well placed in the dialogue, can be enough to allow the other to know that the companion is awake, interested and wanting to hear more, without in any way impeding the process. They can also be helpfully non-committal, implying neither assent nor disapproval but simply indicating attentiveness.

Verbal responses

Sometimes, of course, a verbal response will be appropriate, and these give opportunities to stimulate the flow, perhaps to clarify uncertain points, to assure the other that they are being heard and understood, or to help the other to assimilate what they themselves have said. Let's look at a few examples.

Reflection

In conversations about listening, references to the technique of reflection frequently include the words 'and paraphrasing', which we shall consider in a moment. Both are useful techniques, but they fulfil somewhat different purposes and should not be confused. Reflecting is the direct use of a word or phrase that the other has employed. It could be said, in railway terms, to be the Clapham Junction of listening skills – one can (or certainly once could, at any rate) go just about anywhere from Clapham Junction! Perhaps an example would clarify that extravagant claim.

Suppose the other says, 'We're off to Blackpool next week.'

The companion might respond with the single word, 'Blackpool.'

The other may then take the conversation in one of various directions, for example:

- 'Yes – Blackpool! We used to go there every year but haven't been since the drowning accident.'
- 'That's where I popped the question – might be a chance to rekindle some romance after all these years, you never know.'
- 'Every bloomin' year we do it – Joan's got this thing about the illuminations – don't get it myself – give me the Lake District any day.'
- 'Yes – not that the place matters – I just hate going away.'
- 'Well, yes, Blackpool. But it's next week – that's the problem!'

Each of those responses might then open up a serious issue that's in the mind of the other, without it having been steered in any way by assumptions on the part of the companion. That last response, indeed, might prompt another reflection from the companion – 'Next week' – which is very likely to provide an opening for the other to expand on the real heart of the issue.

I am reminded of an occasion when I used this technique for different reasons. On entering an in-patient ward I was approached by a patient I had not seen before who, as I soon began to realise, suffered from a thought disorder that expressed itself in torrents of speech with changes of subject every few words, so that it was impossible to discern any coherent theme. For a while, I was quite thrown by the confrontation and at a loss to know what to do. Clearly, it mattered to the patient that I listened to him – and I guessed, correctly as it turned out, that few people ever gave him the time except to taunt him for his symptoms. For what seemed like hours – probably a couple of minutes in reality – I stood there in the ward reception area, listening to him and randomly reflecting words: 'Lorry.' 'Potatoes.' 'Computer.' 'Slippers.'

I did not know where this might lead but suspected it would be nowhere, and part of me was wondering how on earth I was ever going to bring the conversation to a close – which clearly I was going to have to do, but the patient, having at long last found someone to listen, was sure to resist. After what seemed an eternity, the ward manager approached the patient. 'I'm really sorry to interrupt, but I need a quick word with the chaplain – is that OK?'

Later, the manager said to me, 'You may wonder what all that was about, but I'll tell you this: that man will never forget the person who stood and showed that he was listening.'

The manager was proved correct when, years later, I bumped into the same patient in a different place. As soon as he saw me his face lit up and he made a beeline for me. I remembered the routine well, and this time slipped into it as to the manner born. 'Railway.' 'Waterfall.' 'Garage.' 'Roses . . .'

In some ways, that might seem patronising – there was a sense in which I was giving the appearance of listening and perhaps even of understanding, when in truth I had no idea what he was really trying to say to me. However, his response made very clear that the mere fact of being heard was what really mattered to him. Being understood would have been good, too – but just being accorded the respect of being given time and attention had its own value. And the reflections told him he had had that. Sometimes – probably most of the time, in fact – our imperfect best has to be enough.

Paraphrasing

This is a very powerful way of assuring the other that they have been heard, as well as checking out that we have correctly understood them. It differs from reflection in that it specifically concentrates on using *different* words to express what they have said.

Other: He never consults me about anything. Last week he went out and bought a new car without a word to me first – and it's not like we've got money to

	burn! I sometimes wonder whether I matter at all – he obviously doesn't think my opinion counts for anything.
Companion:	You feel devalued when he makes serious decisions without consulting you.

Sometimes, paraphrasing might be used in a tentative way in order to check that we have understood, and also in order to show respect to the other in that we are not assuming that our understanding is correct but are actively offering them the opportunity to correct us where necessary. A simple upward inflection, implying a question, would give the response above that added value, or it might be appropriate – occasionally – to make it more explicit: 'Can I just check that I've understood . . . ?'

Of course, making every paraphrase into a question could become tiresome and convey to the other that their pastoral companion is lacking confidence – again, it's about using the skills sensitively and learning from experience. A kind of sixth sense does develop over time.

Of course, all verbal responses should be used economically: it is important not to be constantly interrupting the flow but to give the other time to open up. That particularly applies to the third of these techniques.

Summarising

This is something that might well be helpful, not only in showing that we are listening and understanding but also in helping to bring order into chaos. When the other is going through a particularly stressful or painful time, they may well be experiencing a confusing, even bewildering, array of feelings that they find hard to define, and the pastoral conversation may well take a number of twists and turns. It is easy for the companion to become as disoriented as the other – perhaps even more so since the former is on unfamiliar ground.

Occasionally summarising the conversation – or the most recent part of it – can be very helpful. It gives the other an opportunity to correct anything we have not quite heard clearly and again shows the other that we are not only paying attention but also actively processing what we hear. But it has another advantage in helping the other to see more clearly the components of what may be a very chaotic and messy world that, from their viewpoint at the centre of it, feels quite threatening. The companion's viewpoint is different in many ways and they may well be in a position to clarify by summarising what has been said so far.

Would it be OK if I try and sum up what you've told me so far – maybe to make sure I've got this much of it right? There seem to be a number of things that are really important to you: there's your daughter's marriage difficulties where you wish you could do more to support her and her family; you've told me about the changes at work and that you feel insulted by having to reapply for your own job yet again; and you mentioned a dilemma about your health – part of you wants to get the pains checked out and the other part of you is naturally scared of what you might find. Is that a fair summary of what you've told me so far?

The important thing about a summary is that it should be just that: a succinct highlighting of the main points of the conversation rather than a laboured repetition of its details (which would probably serve only to increase confusion). The other might well have told the companion many other things about the details of these issues and their effects on, for example, their partner and colleagues, and it has all seemed something of a tangle that appears impossible to sort out. The companion, from their different vantage point, and with the benefit of coming fresh to the scene, may well be better placed to identify and categorise the main headings in this way. It might well be that the other, caught up in not only the facts but the anxieties they present, has been mentally flashing back and forth between one thing and another and they have never really been able to recognise that what appear to be a thousand and one issues actually do boil down to just a few. These few words from their pastoral companion may be just what they needed in order to get things a little more into proportion and begin to address them.

Silence

It would be a mistake, though, in thinking about an active presence, to confuse silence with inactivity. I suggested at the beginning of this section a number of ways in which we can demonstrate our attentiveness and encourage the other's internal processing without using words. We also need to recognise that sometimes a quiet stillness is the best possible thing to offer. The other might have come to this meeting from a frenetic and hyperactive environment where just being still and quiet is an unaffordable luxury. It may even be that they feel guilty about 'doing nothing' and so deny themselves the serenity that something deeper within them is craving. The companion can not only provide a helpful context but may even, in doing so, also 'model' to the other that this is OK.

While writing this book, I came across these words about the value of silence:

> There is such a difference between 'being silenced' and 'finding the silence beyond words'. Enforced silence limits us from our full potential. We were born to speak, to sing, to laugh and to find our own voice. And only when all this has begun to come to fruition can we find the rich, deep listening place, a place beyond words. I am just discovering this place, not through silent retreat or Ignatian spirituality, but rather in the opening up of a listening space both around me and within me. In this deep absence of words there is a profound sense of being heard. It is not a comfortable place, it brings lament as well as laughter, but within it I am discovering an infinite sense of the creator listening to the whole of creation, including me![11]

If the silence becomes noticeably uncomfortable – probably because it is unfamiliar and both parties are anxious about how the other is finding it – then it might be helpful, quietly and briefly, to mention that: 'We've both gone rather quiet. I'm quite comfortable with that if you are – just take whatever time you need.'

Sometimes what start off as fairly brief – and uncomfortable – silences change over a number of meetings to become longer and deeply appreciated.

During my counselling training, one of the student group was clearly struggling with the experience of silences. Well, actually, I strongly suspect we all were, but she had the courage and integrity to articulate it. After trying in vain to elicit a comforting response from the tutor, she said, 'But what do you do when simply *nothing* is happening?'

The simple, memorable reply from tutor Alan Frankland was, 'It is impossible for two people to be together and "nothing" be happening.'

When skills disappear

A vital thing to recognise is that none of these 'techniques' is a magic formula. Indeed, while it's good to understand some basic skills, they should not be uppermost in our minds when we are engaging with another. Inevitably, less-experienced companions will be more aware of them, but gradually the attention will focus much more on the other and on the relationship.

---

11 Glasson, Barbara, *Finding a Way* (Kevin Mayhew 2015) p.14.

I remember a very fine musician saying to me how his instrument 'disappeared' when he was performing. It may seem a strange idea, but from my own experience as a lesser musician it is actually a very good description. The skills and techniques have been instilled and absorbed, the technical difficulties of particular works have been practised until they are completely 'under the fingers', and the performer has made the skills so much a part of their being that all they need to be aware of is the music as all else 'disappears', allowing complete concentration on the artistry. This contrasts strongly with the experience of the less-proficient player for whom there is always an awareness of the technical demands of the piece, even in a concert performance.

In the same way, for an inexperienced pastoral companion or counsellor, it is easy to become preoccupied with the techniques, but as we become more practised we find that they 'disappear' as our attention focuses on the other and the skills come into play easily, naturally and to a large extent unconsciously when they are appropriate. The skills are, after all, no more than a means to an end – which is the well-being of the other.

What we have really been considering here is how we can ensure that our way of being present is helpful to the other – which includes enabling them to have confidence that we truly are present to them. However, we should not lose sight of the insight with which we began this exploration.

You may perhaps remember Edgar, the rabbit we met at the start of this book? Having spent some time considering the active aspects of listening, it may be no bad thing to remind ourselves of the basic point – the potential value of simply being there.

During my counselling training, we were required (with the clients' permission, of course) to present audio- and video-tapes of real counselling sessions for assessment by the university assessors. Naturally, not all clients were willing, and that was absolutely respected, but a good number were open to this once they had been assured of the safeguards that were in place. One of my clients who was very cooperative seemed at first to be somewhat unpromising material. During her sessions, she spoke almost constantly, giving me little opportunity to display the impressive array of counselling skills of which I hoped to provide evidence for the assessment. She also had an uncanny way of anticipating my interventions and pre-empting them – so as soon as I thought of something to say that would sound really impressive on the tape and help me accumulate brownie points from the assessor, I would hear her saying it – sometimes in the exact words that were forming in my mind.

What I gradually noticed, however, was that there seemed to be a progression in her train of thought. Although (because?) I had little or no opportunity to have any influence, it usually seemed at the end of the session that she had made a journey, and in a helpful direction. I had not heard of Edgar at that time, but I did come to understand the process in a similar way, and decided to submit for assessment a recording of one of our sessions. The assessment was essentially positive. The assessor commented that it was clear that the client was benefiting from the presence of the student counsellor in enabling her to articulate and 'hear' her own thoughts more clearly.

This is underpinned by Val Wosket, who writes:

> Most of us have had clients who appear to need us to do little more than sit and listen to their stories and yet who clearly experience our listening as significantly therapeutic.[12]

In my case, the assessor did mention, though, that a few of the interventions I managed to shoehorn into the dialogue sounded like the products of my own fevered desperation to be heard to be 'doing something', in spite (rather than because) of which the client found the session helpful. It is supremely important not to lose sight of this in all the consideration of skills and interventions that clearly has to take place here. Sometimes the simplest approaches are the best.

A facilitative presence

Some people live in such dysfunctional worlds that they come to believe (consciously or otherwise) that they are not 'allowed' to have positive experiences. Psychotherapy has a range of techniques for addressing this, but there's really nothing to compare with actually having a positive experience. Sometimes it may be that we can enable such an experience by some very simple measures that lie within our remit (I am not here thinking about booking the other on a flight to Disneyland!). An example of this, amounting simply to a change of venue, comes readily to mind.

The client – a long-stay patient – used to meet me in a therapy room at the mental health in-patient unit that had for decades been her second home. At first we followed the standard practice, sitting in a therapy room while she talked and I listened as empathically as I was able. However, I became aware that I was not being as helpful as I might be. Whatever was said in the room, she needed more: she needed to *experience hope* in tangible ways – the hope that she might one day enjoy life again. And the best way to facilitate

---

12 Wosket, Val, *The Therapeutic Use of Self* (Routledge 1999), p.34.

that was to expose her to enjoyable experiences. The opportunity was there for me to do that by incorporating into our time together her habit of taking a regular walk around the perimeter of the hospital buildings.

So it was that one day I suggested we go for a stroll in the grounds – and did she know that the complex included a sensory garden? As we walked, we continued the counselling session, but with important differences. She caught the scents of various herbs and spices growing there, began to see more vividly the variety of colours, ran her fingers over the varied tactile surfaces and heard the sound of running water from the specially installed feature. She began to experience herself differently – not as a client receiving counselling from a therapist, but as a *person* walking with a companion in a beautiful place and *enjoying* her environment. It also helped her to think of counselling differently. We were exploring some very dark and scary territory, and it is far from unknown for clients to begin to absent themselves from sessions. They feel (often rightly) that they are actually moving into dangerous areas and, as far as they can see, things are getting worse, not better. My intention here was not, in a simplistic way, to make the counselling enjoyable for her – I knew it could never be that – but to give her a glimmer of hope that she might one day be able to enjoy pleasant experiences.

That hope is vital as the early stages of the counselling journey proceed – something I shall say more about when we come to look at biblical material in chapters 5 to 9.

I should say that these positive experiences were not any kind of silver bullet. Even after this, the threats remained and the client did indeed absent herself from occasional sessions when things were really tough, and even continued in her attempts to end her life, as we all realistically expected. However, the value of the positive experiences was very real to her and certainly played a part in her eventually being able to find a significant degree of healing.

In supervision, I reflected on our use of the garden. My supervisor commented that it was, within her own model, unorthodox, but went on, 'You are uniting two roles – that of a traditional pastor in a church and a counsellor in a structured clinical environment – and bringing insights and practices from both to bear on your work. I don't have a problem with that.'

As the benefits became apparent we started to look beyond the hospital grounds to other local beauty spots, including a canal towpath where we would walk as far as the tea rooms, enjoy a cup of tea and then walk back. These sessions happened occasionally, as breaks from the more usual counselling setting, sometimes using the latter to reflect on the different self-concept that was beginning – slowly and often painfully – to emerge.

After the client's discharge from the ward, I introduced her to a socio-therapeutic group run by our volunteer department, and that decision led to a pivotal and hugely significant moment when the group – with myself among the staff – went on a theatre visit and I heard her laugh for the first time. I knew the significance of that: she had often looked back wistfully to happier days, remembering a life filled with laughter, firmly believing that those days were past and unable to entertain any other possibility. She had not laughed since the tragedy, some years earlier, that had eventually led her to me.

The point about all this, of course, is that she *experienced* these positive things. However, it's important not to be simplistic about this. The formal counselling remained important: we needed not only to reflect on these moments in a neutral environment but also to continue to explore the other issues that were part of her very complex case. Nonetheless, there is no doubt in my mind that enabling those experiences played a vital part in – and indeed considerably shortened – the overall process.

She still struggles – there was and will be no quick fix for her long-standing mental health issues – but now, several years after ending therapy, she is able to function, to cope with the bad times and enjoy the good, in ways that had previously seemed impossible not only to her but also to some of the most respected clinicians I knew.

And she laughs. Not as often as she'd like, but laugh she does – something that she had thought was no longer possible, even in her dreams.

A disappointing presence

Something often acknowledged by therapists is also applicable (although to a lesser extent) to pastoral companions: we must expect sometimes to disappoint our others – and the subject of this book is one of the prime reasons for that. While the pastoral companion is in a different role from the counsellor, the expectations can be similar. We noted earlier the popular misconception of the counsellor as the wise and powerful being who can make things right, and it is quite likely that someone seeking help from a minister or pastoral companion might have similar perceptions of the process.

One of the qualities any pastoral companion needs is the strength to resist the pressure of expectations – along with the ability to be with the other in the disappointment experienced and to continue to be trusted through it. It can be quite undermining of the companion's confidence to know that the other is hoping for – even demanding –

some kind of positive action or guidance, and the temptation to give in to that can be almost overwhelming, but it must be resisted.

This issue will be explored both explicitly and in the subtext of this book, but it seems important to acknowledge it early on because one of the first priorities of any helping relationship is clarity of expectation. 'Contracting'[13] is the first and an ongoing task in a formal counselling relationship, and takes at least two forms. As well as covering matters such as fees, cancellations, time, place, frequency and duration of sessions – some but not all of which may also be appropriate in less-formal contexts – it also would include conversations about expectations. What does the other hope to gain? What do they expect of the companion? What responsibilities should each feel towards the other? And so on. Having once had the conversation, it may well be necessary to revisit elements of it during sessions to reclarify where responsibility lies and what is or is not within the companion's remit.

Clarity of expectation is particularly essential in pastoral companionship as the lines are more blurred. A counsellor in a clinical practice, for example, will not expect to meet with a client outside the agreed parameters, whereas a pastoral companion or a minister in a church will undoubtedly see the other at worship, at the coffee mornings and in many other settings. This factor can be a serious complication, confusing expectations and placing the pastoral carer under additional pressure.

Another complication is that a counsellor is only engaged with the actual client – not the client's partner, parents, children, etc. In a church context, the pastoral companion is almost certainly going to have some kind of relationship with some or all of those, and they are likely to make their presence felt in one way or another along the shared journey.

All these factors will affect the expectations placed upon the companion, and it is essential to be able to manage the pressures, along with the anxieties and disappointments that they engender. We shall look at some of the issues this involves in the final chapter, but my main concern at this stage is that the pastoral companion must be clear about what can be expected of them and have the confidence and the support to deal with the sense of disappointment (actual or perceived) that easily can and probably will arise.

We have been exploring ways of being present to another that actively facilitate healing and growing processes. What would now be helpful would be to consider in a little more depth what some of those processes are, and how the respectful presence of a companion may enable them.

---

13 As mentioned earlier, this does not necessarily mean a formal written document – although in some situations it will – but may be just a short conversation held on first meeting, to be returned to as necessary on later occasions, in which the fair expectations of both sides are made clear.

3
Counselling insights

Having been clear from the start that this is not a counselling manual, we should still expect some insights from the counselling world to be helpful in the work of a pastoral companion. There is a vital distinction between a 'counsellor', which in terms of the current discussion means something quite specific, and a 'user of counselling skills' – a term often employed to describe people whose work (professional or voluntary) involves using some of the skills that are associated with counselling but in a less specific context.

Perhaps it would be good to begin with some clarification of the distinction between the two. Counselling, for these purposes, would be defined as a service provided by appropriately qualified professionals, within a structured environment, according to commonly accepted criteria, following an agreed set of ethical and good-practice guidelines, under structured supervision provided by appropriately qualified personnel and with clear disciplinary and complaints procedures to protect the clientele.

It will readily be apparent that much highly valuable work is done, especially in faith communities, that is of a more informal nature, and for which the necessary training and qualifications are different (although some of the above criteria might well apply in varying degrees according to circumstance). It is here that the work of the pastoral companion would generally sit. The aim of this section of the book is to enable that work to be illuminated by some of the insights, developed through research, that inform counselling practice.

It would be possible to draw upon many different theoretical models for this, but I propose to concentrate on the one which is my particular field: the person-centred approach (PCA).

What follows is a very quick thumbnail sketch covering just a few of the principles and insights of the PCA that are helpful to us here; it is light years from being an exhaustive or comprehensive treatment of the subject.

The person-centred approach to counselling and psychotherapy

This approach grew out of the work of the American psychologist Carl Rogers in the 1950s. It is sometimes referred to as 'non-directive' counselling because Rogers specifically excluded any idea that the counsellor was in a position to direct or steer the client, believing rather, as has already been suggested, that the counsellor's role was to provide a psychological environment in which the client would be encouraged and enabled to find their own direction. Rogers, however, while not changing his fundamental view, came to regard the non-directive tag as an ideal that he thought was (although desirable) pretty well unattainable. The process that develops between two people in relationship is more complex and subtle than that would suggest and he came to the belief that, try as we might, it is probably not possible for one person to enable another without – at least in some small way – having an effect on the direction they take.

For some years the approach was known as client-centred therapy, but this too was to change as Rogers and his colleagues developed their thinking and learnt from their research. There are, of course, not one but two persons in the process, and the counsellor needs to be aware not only of what is happening in and for the client but also what is happening within the counsellor him or herself and – crucially – how the inner processes of both are affecting each other and their relationship. And so the thinking began to shift away from client-centricity and towards the *person*-centred approach. The importance of this insight will become much clearer when we come to consider the 'core conditions' for a helping relationship.

I do not propose to embark here upon a detailed exposition of person-centred personality theory, but rather I shall focus upon one particular component of that which seems to me to be of fundamental significance as we consider the healing power of presence.

The actualising tendency

This was Rogers' term for the drive towards growth and fulfilment that he derived initially from his observation of the potato in the cellar (see 'Consider the potato' in chapter 1). He developed the theory that this drive is present in all living organisms and can only be stopped by death:

> We are, in short, dealing with an organism which is always seeking, always initiating, always 'up to something.' There is one central source of energy in the human organism. It is a trustworthy function of the whole system rather than of some portion of it.[14]

---

14   Rogers, Carl R., *The Foundations of the Person-Centred Approach* (1979) p.5.

Rogers was at pains to make clear that the drive is not simply for self-preservation but for growth and development – a push toward increasing complexity. While the tendency cannot be stopped, it can, as I observed earlier, be misdirected and become unhealthy if the environment (physical or psychological) is not helpful. This, Rogers concluded, was the fate that had befallen the potato which, in the absence of what it needed for healthy growth, continued to strive for its own development and became distorted in the process.

Personality theory offers various insights into just why and how this happens, some of which will be touched upon at points where it is considered to be helpful to this exploration. It is enough for now to acknowledge that generally the causes lie in the way we relate to other people, especially in our formative years. The focus of the person-centred approach, therefore, is upon the use of healthy, facilitative relationship as the main instrument of healing. The aim is not to heal or to change the other, but rather to *enable* healing and positive change by providing the conditions in which their own actualising tendency can work unhindered.

The conditions for therapeutic change

From their research, Rogers and his colleagues identified six conditions that they said must be present in a relationship for healing to take place, and three of these were identified as the 'core conditions' at the heart of the process. We shall explore those now and, at the risk of repeating myself, we shall do so in recognition that what follows is a very simple treatment. Each of these conditions has occupied countless pages in textbooks and research findings. However, as long as we are aware of that, we might uncover enough to help us understand a little better the process in which we, as pastoral companions, are involved.

The core conditions are: congruence, empathy and the rather jargonesque 'unconditional positive regard'. Don't be put off by the jargon, but let us take those three in turn.

Congruence

In a counselling relationship the ideal is for the counsellor to be in a state of 'congruence'. Essentially, this means that there is a consistency between what the counsellor is feeling and what is happening deep inside. Perhaps the easiest way to clarify this is with an example.

Many years ago, during a residential training event for ministers, I found myself experiencing extremely (and quite inexplicably) negative feelings towards another member of the course. It would have been very easy to have placed responsibility for those feelings on the other person, but that did not make sense as we had had no real contact. I found his presence – or rather, my feelings towards him – so distracting that I had to take time apart to consider what was happening within me.

It did not take long for the reasons for my antipathy to emerge. The person concerned bore a striking resemblance to a work colleague from an earlier chapter of my life whom I had found difficult in a number of ways. In particular, that person had seemed to go out of his way to belittle others and generally convey a sense of his own superiority – something that had been felt not just by me but by many others in that workplace. The effect was made worse by the fact that he actually was very good at his job (and in truth I learned a great deal from him – even if reluctantly), but instead of feeling respect towards him, my response was to feel devalued in myself. All the associated feelings had now been rekindled by the quite innocent and unknowing presence of someone who strongly resembled him physically (but was, as it turned out, a very different personality).

During our early encounters on the course it could be said that I was 'in a state of incongruence'. I was responding to my conscious feelings but was not aware of the internal process that was generating them – there was no 'congruence' between the two. It would have been easy to voice my feelings in terms of, 'He makes me feel . . .', when in fact he was doing nothing to contribute to my distress. It would have been too easy to take in all my experience of this gentleman through the filters of my past – to see him (to use a slightly different metaphor) through the lens of my earlier experience. Indeed, that is exactly what I *had* found myself doing – and it could easily have resulted in very unpleasant misunderstandings for us both. Recognising the process happening within me – which I later came to know as transference[15] – enabled me to move from incongruence to 'a state of congruence' in relation to my new colleague as I owned the cause of those feelings as being within me and not with him. I was able then to recognise and begin to deal with the issues that I had been unwittingly projecting on to him.

It's not hard to see the relevance of this to a counselling or pastoral companionship situation. A significant proportion of the difficulty we experience in relationships generally is about this kind of process: things people say, the way they stand, the clothes they wear, their

---

15 The direction towards someone else of feelings that rightly relate to a third party – a concept that is well known and which plays a central role in dynamic psychotherapy.

physical appearance – all these and much more can evoke feelings within us that we can too easily attribute to them but may well have completely separate origins (not necessarily transference, although that is one possibility). One way of alerting ourselves to this is to change the way we express our feelings to ourselves:

'This guy really makes me feel sick,' becomes, 'Why is that I feel sick when I'm with this person?'

'She's really making me angry,' becomes, 'Why am I feeling angry towards this person?'

Of course, it may be that our feelings are, in simple terms, justified: if someone is expressing odious racist sentiments, for example, then anger might be an appropriate response. However, if we reflect upon it we might find a better way of dealing with it than is suggested by our gut, as well as become aware of other more subtle components within the mixture of causes – and it is almost always a mixture.

In the case of this example, the next question would be about the other: 'Why would someone have feelings like this?' That is indeed an excellent question to ask. People do not adopt offensive or threatening views for no reason, and they do not grow into apparently unattractive or repellent personalities because they want to do so. As well as being open to the deeper processes within ourselves (undoubtedly the first and crucial consideration), we need to find ways behind the outward presentation and enter insofar as we are able into the world of the other.

And that is our next topic.

Empathy

Empathy is a word that 'everyone knows' and many use, but it might be fair to say that relatively few truly understand. It is widely taken to mean a more intense kind of sympathy, but in fact the two are very different.

Sympathy can hold great dangers in that the companion can become submerged in the other's feelings and the two end up drowning together. That is not only dangerous but also disrespectful as the other's feelings are misappropriated by the companion who may feel – and perhaps claim – that they share them. The classic example is, 'I know how you feel,' which is often said with the intention of offering comfort and conveying empathy, but in fact can feel very alienating. Who does this person think they are in claiming insight into my deep feeling? How can anyone know how another feels? Every human person and relationship is unique, and even if experiences are identical, people will respond in significantly (even if only slightly) different ways.

As well as appearing patronising, the claim can also have the effect of shutting out the other. If you already know how I'm feeling then there's not much point in my telling you. If I already know how you're feeling then I don't really need to listen – I may hear some of what you say but obviously I'll be able to complete sentences for you in my own head and apply my own understandings and interpretations where you're struggling to express yourself. In short – accurate listening goes out of the window.

Empathy is *not* compassion with knobs on! In fact, it might be said that it is not (at least in its early stages) an emotional thing at all. It is a conscious effort of will, by which we enter into the internal world of another. As Barrett-Lennard expresses it:

> Empathy . . . is a form of enquiring and knowing, a caring *but disciplined* opening of self to the lived feelings of the other.[16]

Barrett-Lennard goes on to emphasise the otherness aspect and the importance of the therapist's awareness of that – what we earlier saw described by Placher as 'to look the other honestly in the face'.

Empathy, then, is a *disciplined* mental exercise. Done well, it will of course result in our experiencing feelings similar to those of the client, but those feelings are not ours; they belong to the client, and a truly empathic companion will recognise and respect that.

A helpful description of empathy that I found spoke in terms of being able to enter the internal world of the other and move around in it as if it were our own, but 'always remembering the "as if".' Unfortunately I cannot now find the reference for it, but it impressed me very much as a succinct and clear definition.

Frames of reference

It is appropriate here briefly to allude to the concept of 'frames of reference'. Each of us, inescapably, views the world from within a particular frame of reference that has been constructed over our lifetime from the experiences we have had. It will be immediately apparent that every individual's frame of reference is bound to be unique, which means at least two things.

Firstly, our experience is *interpreted* experience – we are seeing, hearing and feeling through the filters of our past experiences and relationships: our 'frame of reference'.

---

16 Barrett-Lennard, Godfrey T., *Carl Rogers' Helping System, Journey and Substance* (Sage 1998), p.81, emphasis mine.

Secondly, the same experience will be interpreted differently (even if only slightly) by another who is viewing it from within a different frame of reference. Empathy requires that the companion remains aware of what is in the other's frame of reference and what is in their own. It includes the ability to leave that world and return to one's own frame of reference as and when it becomes necessary. This is important both in terms of respect for the other and care of the self. Becoming so absorbed in the other's predicament as to find oneself in effect trapped in their frame of reference would be deeply damaging to the companion personally, and would also seriously endanger the effectiveness of the work with the other – which is just one of many reasons why we must make the vital distinction between empathy and sympathy.

Unconditional positive regard (UPR)

It is not at all uncommon for people to deride this term as jargon – but I am reluctant to do that. Like empathy, unconditional positive regard (UPR) needs to be clearly distinguished from other qualities that could become confused with it. Crucially, we do not need to like someone or approve of their behaviour in order to offer them UPR.

Rogers, who coined the term, also used words like 'warmth' and 'prizing'. The last is significant – we can 'prize' without actually liking! Daily I see things that I really cannot say I like, but I recognise that they are of worth. If someone were to entrust to my care a possession of enormous sentimental value, I would 'prize' it as much as the privilege of such trust – but that would not depend upon my liking it as an artefact. Experience convinces me that it is very possible to recognise the value of a human being even when all that is in us is repelled by their presentation. This raises difficult issues, and for many it *seems* to conflict with congruence – but there are ways we can help ourselves to bridge the gap.

Unconditional is the key word

For many people – probably all of us to some extent or another – the positive regard we have received from others has more often been conditional than unconditional. We might have had the feeling that it would be – has been – withheld if we have not met some requirement or other. As a result, we have introjected others' demands upon us as 'conditions of worth' – standards that we must meet in order to be of value. Let's think about those, first.

Conditions of worth

I was fortunate to grow up in a home that was characterised to an extraordinary degree by unconditional love. Looking back on those happy times, and reflecting on them with my family and others who visited us and also sensed it, it is very clear that we did not need to earn our parents' love. Sadly, that is not something that is necessarily the case for all children – and even if it is, they may see things differently.

For all that I *was* loved unconditionally, I did not always *experience* it that way at the time. For some reason that is still not clear, I struggled at school and often found it difficult to grasp the apparently obvious. Many of my teachers were at a loss either to understand or to help. My father's very natural anxiety about this, and his emphasis on the importance of educational success – all born out of his deep love for his children and the earnest desire that we be enabled to live happy and satisfying lives – were interpreted by me as, in effect, conditions of worth. Recognising that my educational progress was highly important to my father (which it was), I came to think of it as a condition of his love (which it most emphatically was not). Then in a more general sense I began to associate academic success with personal worth – something that even now my heart still sometimes feels even though my head knows better! As I look back now, I know that I could not possibly have been loved more fully or more unconditionally than I was, but even then I still felt the need for approval. How much more, then, must this be the case for those from less idyllic backgrounds in which the 'love' offered really was highly conditional.

Whether deliberately imposed on us or introjected by us through misunderstandings, conditions of worth are surely part of all our experience. It would be remarkable if, in our family, friendships, education and employment, we had never been made to feel (or have mistakenly felt – congruence again!) that our value was dependent upon meeting someone else's standards.

So we probably all experience positive regard as conditional, and in many people the resulting introjection of conditions of worth mean that they never really feel able to risk letting their true self be known. Instead, they adopt a 'self-concept' that is shaped by those conditions of worth and which they not only present to the world but also, crucially, *come to believe in for themselves*. This is understandable – we do not want to be living a lie, so will want to convince not only others but also ourselves that our 'self-concept' is real. More to the point, if we have truly introjected those conditions of worth, we shall have adopted them as our criteria and will desperately want to believe that we meet them. So it is that the 'self-concept' comes to be regarded by us as the 'self'.

The experience of being unconditionally accepted – which we may take a long time to come to believe – can be vital in enabling us to feel that we can reveal (to ourselves as much as to others) more of the real self within. As Barrett-Lennard expresses it:

The interactive quality of unconditional positive regard [is] theoretically pivotal in undoing conditions of worth.[17]

From this very brief treatment of the subject, we can imagine that UPR is fundamental to the healing power of presence. If we can enable the other to perceive that they do not need to meet our conditions in order to be valued, then they may begin to feel more confident to allow the masks to slip and begin to reveal the true self hidden behind. As they find that what is revealed is respected, so they feel able to show more. Along with that goes the slowly growing confidence to accept themselves as they truly are. This is the essential core of the process of healing and of becoming. I have worked with people well into their retirement years who were powerfully enabled by UPR to reveal aspects of themselves they had hidden since childhood.

However, there is a serious stumbling block to all this. I am often challenged by people with the question, 'But how can you value a violent criminal or a sex offender? Surely you can't genuinely like them – and if you can't, will you have to pretend? What price congruence, then?'

UPR and congruence: the Odd Couple?

A question that frequently occupies students of the person-centred approach concerns the conflict between UPR and congruence when working with certain types of people. It's a good question – and to a large extent it's helped by a more accurate understanding of one or other of those core conditions.

Frequently, congruence is confused with honesty, which is dangerous because it can become an excuse for self-indulgence: 'I've got to be congruent, so I have to tell you that I find you repulsive. Sorry, but I'd be incongruent if I didn't tell you.'

As will be understood from the short exploration earlier in this chapter, that is a terrible misrepresentation of congruence. It is not a matter of congruence between what I feel and what I say, but between what I feel and *what is going on at a deeper level within me*. So,

---

17 Barrett-Lennard, *Carl Rogers' Helping System, Journey and Substance*, p.81.

assuming that I find someone repulsive, the congruent response to that, as we have seen already, is not to blurt it out but to ask myself the question, 'What is it about me that produces that response to this person?' There is all the difference in the world between 'She is repulsive' and 'I find her repulsive'.

Along with that must go the ability to make clear distinctions between the person and the behaviours, between objective worth and subjective appeal. We all know of instances where what seem to us very strange and even unattractive artworks have been hailed as priceless by the cognoscenti and sold for what some of us might consider ridiculous amounts of money. Some famous examples spring readily to mind: a pile of bricks, an unmade bed, half a cow preserved in formaldehyde. To me, those range from plain boring to repulsive, and I am tempted to question whether they even qualify as art. But I cannot deny the evidence that others – who do not otherwise appear to be bereft of reason – have recognised immense value in them. The fact that I personally find them objectionable does not necessarily imply that those others are mistaken. It could very well be that I am.

My unconditional valuing of other people is not based (by definition, it could not be) on whether I like them, or even whether I see evidence of their value, but upon a vitally important principle that has been expressed many times in terms of equality of birth:

> All [people] are born free and equal, and have certain natural, essential, and unalienable rights.[18]

Unlike the well-known USA Declaration of Independence, the Massachusetts declaration does not appeal to any religious beliefs but simply says that we are all born equal, with certain rights. Crucially, it does not say (because it is not relevant) that all people are good, likeable, pretty or intelligent! Of course, the idea is frequently linked to religious belief, which I shall look at in more detail later when considering the Genesis creation stories in chapter 5, but the point here is that one does not need to be a theist in order to believe in the intrinsic value of each human person. The way a person behaves might very well be quite another matter, but it does not negate the value which is there intrinsically as part of their essential make-up. It is born with every one of us.

Sometimes – actually quite often in my specialist field – I would be working with others who had behaved in ways that they later found embarrassing or shameful. I would try to assure them that I was not actually interested in judging the behaviour, only in exploring the

---

18 Article 1 of the Declaration of Rights of the Massachusetts Constitution.

reasons for it. People do not do bizarre or objectionable things for no reason, and trying to understand the reason is likely to be more helpful than judging the behaviour – and more likely, where that is appropriate, to change it, too. The reasons for those behaviours were quite separate from the people's own worth; they were not born in them but rather had been accumulated by their interaction with the world. As William Wordsworth expressed it:

> Our birth is but a sleep and a forgetting:
> The Soul that rises with us, our life's Star,
> Hath had elsewhere its setting,
> And cometh from afar:
> Not in entire forgetfulness,
> And not in utter nakedness,
> But trailing clouds of glory do we come
> From God, who is our home:
> Heaven lies about us in our infancy!
> Shades of the prison-house begin to close
> Upon the growing Boy,
> But He beholds the light, and whence it flows,
> He sees it in his joy;
> The Youth, who daily farther from the east
> Must travel, still is Nature's Priest,
> And by the vision splendid
> Is on his way attended;
> At length the Man perceives it die away,
> And fade into the light of common day.[19]

What we are valuing unconditionally is not the dysfunctional behaviour, conditioned by interaction with the world, but the human person, whose value is a given.

The power of 'as if'

It would be silly of me to pretend that I did not find some of the people with whom I worked seriously unattractive – or, frankly, worse – so here is how I learned to deal with that. I reminded myself that I believe every human being is of infinite worth, and that does not depend on whether I am happy with them or not. So I would treat each person *as if* I found them worthy, even if in my heart of hearts my feelings at that stage were saying something very different. This was not dishonest – and

---

19 Wordsworth, William, 'Ode: Intimations of Immortality (V)' from *Recollections of Early Childhood.*

certainly not incongruent: I was not pretending something, or denying anything, but rather recognising that the feelings I was experiencing did not necessarily reflect the reality of the person in front of me.

So whatever my subjective feelings towards a person, I would always make a conscious effort to *behave as if* I valued them unconditionally. Hopefully, they would experience that as the reality it was (a reality of the head rather than the heart, but a reality all the same), and the potential was then there for the influences of their history to begin to be undone. Sometimes it was powerfully moving to see long-established defences being pulled down like the Berlin Wall, and to observe a person who had been trapped there begin to peer tentatively and sometimes fearfully through the opening. Sometimes, a highly aggressive and volatile 'front' would – slowly and haltingly – begin to give way to the vulnerable, frightened or ashamed soul that it had been erected to protect. It has been my joy and my most treasured privilege to have witnessed that process happening – and too often for it to have been coincidence.

What does this tell us? That the core conditions are effective, certainly – but more than that. My experience has confirmed my belief of the intrinsic value of every human soul, however unlikely that may appear from the outward presentation.

So, then, to sum up: our aim as pastoral companions is to offer to others the healthy psychological environment we have recognised as essential for their becoming. To bring together the particular counselling concepts we have just considered:

> We are seeking, by the quality of our presence, to facilitate for another the kind of psychological environment in which their *actualising tendency* can work to their good and not to their harm, and in doing so to enable it to heal some of the wounds that they carry from the past. For this to happen, we seek to bring to the relationship three *core conditions* that are essential to the process.
>
> We begin with ourselves – aiming to approach the other in a state of *congruence,* aware of our own internal processes and able to relate those to the things we are experiencing in the other – the feelings that arise in us in relation to them.
>
> To the extent that we succeed in this, we are then able to offer them *empathy* as we experience their world from within their *frame of reference* and can sense the feelings that they experience in engaging with it.
>
> Empathy, as distinct from sympathy, allows us to respect their *otherness* and, while able to inhabit their world for whatever time is necessary, to exit from it when it is appropriate to do so.

While we are there, our active listening, expressed particularly in eye contact, minimal encouragers, reflecting, paraphrasing and summarising, will assure the other that they are being heard and understood in a meaningful way, thereby affirming their own worth and the validity of their experience.

In this way they will have the experience of *unconditional positive regard*, effectively undoing *conditions of worth* and allowing them gradually to trust that their true self can be revealed. This allows them to progress in themselves from a state of incongruence to one of congruence as they find the confidence to listen to their own inner processes.

So far we have looked at the concept of 'being there' – of being a helpful presence with another who is in some way in need of help – and we have seen that simply by our presence we can have a powerful effect for good. Having considered that more deeply in terms of the qualities that might characterise our presence, we have then drawn on some of the insights of counselling theory to illuminate the process a little further.

We are now ready to consider how this sits with spirituality – and with Christian spirituality in particular.

4
Spirituality

What is spirituality?

Good question!

'Spirituality' is one of those words that we all use, but we may not realise that we might be talking about quite different things. It is frequently used to mean 'religion', although another speaker may think 'faith' or 'piety', while someone else has in mind tarot cards or healing crystals – to mention just a few of countless possibilities. So it is perhaps no bad thing that we begin with the question of definition.

This immediately presents a problem. In any serious consideration of spiritual matters, simple definitions are inevitably found to be inadequate and need to be qualified in some way, but even then still miss the mark and so demand further qualification. It can be, in the words of one of my line managers, 'like nailing jelly to the wall'. For our purposes here, a more helpful metaphor might be of trying to bottle the breeze or catch the tide in a jar. We would inevitably end up with a jar full of air or water but completely lacking the mysterious energy essential to what we were trying to capture. Sometimes, religions have all too easily fallen into this trap, and when that happens the tragedy is that what is in effect a bottle of thin air or mucky water gets offered to others with the (sometimes genuinely believed) claim that it is spirituality.

The analogies with wind and tide are, I think, good ones (as far as they go): if we want people to experience the beauty and the power of those phenomena, the best we can do is to help them find a place where they can witness them for themselves. And that, for me, is also a pretty good definition of religion at its best: not claiming to have exclusive possession of spirituality or spiritual truth, but offering to others ways of experiencing and exploring those.

It might be said, of course, that the analogies of wind and tide are outdated, springing as they do from times when their causes were not understood and were generally assumed to be manifestations of magical or supernatural power, whereas now we have scientific explanations. To some extent that may be true, but those explanations still do not deprive these phenomena of their mysterious power to affect our well-being; we are still not really sure why the experience of a gentle spring breeze or of watching the ebb and flow of the tide should evoke the feelings of well-being that countless people express. No doubt it is to do with the sense of movement, energy, freedom and so on – all of which, as I observed earlier, are completely lost as soon as they are encapsulated in a container (a 'container' is what any simple definition is very likely to be).

Like the wind and the tide, spirituality is not always gentle and evocative of beautiful feelings; rather it is full of power with immense potential for change, and sometimes that can feel challenging and even threatening. The liberation theologian Jon Sobrino, a Latin American Jesuit priest, has described spirituality as Profound Motivation:[20] it is what fires us up and drives us to try and change things (hopefully for the better) – for some people, at the cost of their own lives. Although I make it in passing, we should not miss the point that spirituality can be a force for harm as well as for good. Just as we do with religion, we need to discern what is good spirituality and what is not.

So as I begin the sixth paragraph in my attempt to define spirituality, I might perhaps claim that the elusiveness of definition is well demonstrated – but I do still need to come to some kind of general idea of what the word represents, if only so that we can move on. Perhaps the answer is not to try to define it at all, but instead to think in terms of its effects, as Jesus did when likening the free movement of the Spirit to the wind (undoubtedly not missing the point that in Hebrew the same word is used for both). This is the approach taken by the Royal College of Psychiatrists:

There is no one definition, but in general, spirituality:

- is something everyone can experience
- helps us to find meaning and purpose in the things we value
- can bring hope and healing in times of suffering and loss
- encourages us to seek the best relationship with ourselves, others and what lies beyond.[21]

That would also be a pretty good understanding of pastoral companionship – and of good counselling or psychotherapy, if it comes to that.

Spirituality and religion

So what, then, is the relationship between spirituality and Christianity – or indeed spirituality and religion in general? It might seem from this chapter so far that I am not really making any connection – so it is time to correct that impression. If spirituality is, as I have suggested,

---

20 I remember reading this in what I regarded as a reliable source, and unfortunately I cannot now recall enough to give an exact reference – but it does sound very Sobrino to me!
21 Royal College of Psychiatrists, 'Spirituality and mental health'. Available at www. rcpsych.ac.uk/mentalhealthinformation/therapies/spiritualityandmentalhealth.aspx (accessed 10 March 2015).

something mysterious and indefinable, then clearly we need a means of organising our way of thinking about it and understanding our experiences. More than that, we need a way of entering into it in order to experience its mysterious power in the first place. Probably from the time *Homo sapiens* became recognisably human – certainly from the time we have been able to articulate our thoughts – religious imagery has been used as a way of contemplating the mysteries we encounter in our beautiful but dangerous environment. So while making a distinction between religion and spirituality, in the hope of not falling into the common trap of seeing them as identical, it is equally important to recognise their common ground.

Let's cut to the chase! The best way I have found of relating them is to think of religion as a way of exploring and expressing spirituality. The religions of the world use stories, historical and otherwise – imagery, metaphor, myth, legend, parable, allegory, all sorts of drama and wisdom writings – to contemplate the infinite mystery that even (or rather especially) in this highly scientific age, many of us still find to be at the heart of life. At its best, religion strives constantly to reach out towards – or simply to express a need for or fascination with – mysterious treasures of beauty and wisdom that are beyond or deep within us. And the fact that we cannot actually grasp them does not stop us from reaching and in that process exploring – and who knows, maybe occasionally just touching something of infinite if inexpressible value.

Religion gets a bad press, and in spite of all the excellent work done by chaplains and other workers it is still sometimes viewed with suspicion in healthcare circles – and mental health particularly. It might be said that this is hardly surprising when some strands of various religions continue to present themselves as an alternative to (or even as the only true) science. Therein is the clue that the real problem is not religion as such but the institutions that can too easily end up as monuments to the spirituality buried deep under the foundations of their structures – an ancient practice of which Jesus accused the institutionally minded Pharisees (Matthew 23:13) but is actually a potential trap for any religion. This, combined with the tendency to use religious labels to identify social and political divisions (e.g. Catholic/Republican, Protestant/Unionist), has not encouraged the perception of religion as a gateway to exploring spirituality. However, the creative heart of religion is not in dogmas and institutions but in story and storytelling.[22]

---

22 It will be objected that religious writings contain much more than stories – they also include much ethical exploration and reflection, for example – but (in the Judaeo-Christian tradition, at any rate) those take place against the background of the story of a faith community, and it is in that story that the power lies.

In writing this book I became once again intensely aware of the power of story in exploring mysterious experiences and ideas. Story does more than describe an event – it awakens our imagination and allows us to connect in new ways with our own selves and histories. Using story as a tool in therapy was something I did initially with a certain sense of danger. Might I be imposing on a client my own interpretation, even my own spirituality or religious belief? Might I be steering a process that should be left to find its own direction? As I used it more, though, I began to feel more comfortable with it as one tool among many in my kit, to be used like any other tool – discriminately and with care. I wish that when I was initially struggling with my doubts I had read Val Wosket's wise observations that, unfortunately, did not show on my radar until retirement approached.

> I became fond of stories at an early age, both through reading and making up my own. I often felt as if I had more real and vibrant relationships with characters in books than with the adults who were around me in my own life. As a counsellor I have retained this absorption in stories . . . Because I find the narratives of my clients vivid and absorbing I have no difficulty listening attentively to them. I sense that I listen well and with interest. I remember details and themes and I naturally conjure up metaphors and images and offer these back to my clients in ways they frequently seem to find useful. It is as if I feed off their stories, enter into, and become a contributor to them.[23]

I remember first reading those words while seated in the reception area of the hospital where I worked, and having almost physically to restrain myself from punching the air and exclaiming, 'Yes! Yes! Yes!', so vivid was the affirmation that I felt for what had seemed a rather unorthodox approach to counselling. (It was, however, quite natural in the context of spiritual and pastoral care, and just one of many examples of working in the border-country between those two different disciplines.)

I share with Wosket the facility to 'conjure up metaphors and images' – and these frequently resonate with images and themes in literature and drama as well as religion. Although sometimes, like Wosket, I have shared these with clients, there have also been some examples that have contributed to my own internal process. One of the valuable aspects of the sharing, when it is appropriate, is in enabling the other to recognise common ground – that while each person's narrative (and the way it is experienced) is unique, it

---

23 Wosket, *The Therapeutic Use of Self*, p.123.

is also grounded in a kind of universality that places us in solidarity with people and peoples down the ages, and they with us. I should emphasise, though, that this is not about simplistically finding solutions to problems – the Bible, like counselling, is not about quick, easy answers – but rather about affecting, often quite subtly, the way we view our own predicaments.

So for the purposes of this book, I'm thinking of religion – and in particular of religious *storytelling* – as a language, a means of expressing and exploring spirituality, by which I mean both spirituality in general and the personal interior spirituality that is each unique person. And it must now become clear that if we are to benefit from this exploration then we must explore without the ambition to possess. This is a prerequisite for any spiritual explorer: we don't march into the realm of spirituality with the flag of some divinely ordained kingdom in our backpack, ready to unfurl it as soon as we have reached our goal. Indeed, there is (in this life at any rate) no final 'goal' to be reached. Rather what might appear to be a destination turns out to be merely a horizon which, when we reach it, we find to be a vantage point for vast new, hitherto-unimagined landscapes that call us irresistibly onward. This is the explorer's experience in the ever-unfolding world of spirituality.

My own particular point of departure for exploring spirituality has always been Christianity – not because I became convinced by intellectual argument that this is 'the True Religion', but because I grew up in a vicarage where I became (creatively) steeped in its traditions from an early age. Christianity is, it might be said, in my blood, and it would seem very strange to begin my quest for spirituality from any other starting point.

Judaeo-Christian spirituality in pastoral companionship

Christian tradition – or more accurately the Judaeo-Christian tradition – offers a wealth of insights that are of immense value to the pastoral companion. I hope here to highlight a selection of those and, more importantly perhaps, to encourage further exploration of other elements in our faith. I believe – and experience bears out – that there are resources here that easily go unnoticed, largely because of the 'tinted lenses' through which they are usually viewed. One of the problems for people steeped in religious traditions and teachings is that we come to read them through the filters of our established beliefs – often knowing not only the Scripture passage itself but the 'correct' interpretation before we begin to read. Too often those lenses can filter out, or simply not encourage us to seek, other layers of meaning. It then becomes very likely that those assumptions are passed on to future generations so that what began as one particular interpretation becomes the accepted standard of faith and – worse – ends up as unquestionable dogma.

So I shall be examining these stories primarily through a different set of lenses, provided by my training and experience not only as a Christian minister but also as a chaplain and counsellor. Not only that, however, I also read them as someone who, like Val Wosket, loves a good story (religious or otherwise) and delights in peeling back the layers of meaning to see what unexpected treasures might emerge and how they resonate with other aspects of life.

This means that I shall be taking a particular approach to the biblical texts. In some of the treatments (such as the creation narratives in Genesis), I believe I am bringing out meanings that were in the minds of the original writers (for which, in many cases, we might read 'communities', as these stories developed in much more communal ways than we sometimes realise).

However, I am also taking another approach – for example, in some of the birth, Passion and resurrection material – in which I seek to make imaginative connection between ancient texts and the current issues we are considering. This is a time-honoured approach, probably as ancient as the written Scriptures themselves, known as midrash. In these instances, I do not claim that my particular application of the texts or the specific insights I draw from them were actually in the minds of the biblical writers, but rather that their writings can be alive for us today in new ways, shedding light upon the questions and needs of our time.

The Hebrew and Christian Scriptures

I propose to begin with the Hebrew Scriptures, generally referred to in Christian circles as the Old Testament, but in fact vibrantly relevant not only to Christian believers but to life in the twenty-first century generally. On the former point, it is often forgotten that what we call the Old Testament was the only Bible Jesus knew and was the source of his own spirituality. It is also a rich source of wisdom and spirituality shared between three great world faiths.[24] So it is particularly unfortunate when in Christian circles the term 'Old

---

24 The three 'religions of the Book' or 'Abrahamic faiths': Judaism, Islam and Christianity. I write as a minister most familiar with Christianity and to a lesser extent Judaism, but with little knowledge of the particularities of Islam and so I am unable to comment on the Islamic interpretations of the passages we shall consider.

Testament' encourages the view of it as somehow less relevant or meaningful or, as is too often said, that the God of the Old Testament is not the God of the New. Sadly, this is apparently endorsed by no less a scholar than John Keble (792–866) in one of his hymns:

When God of old came down from heaven,
in power and wrath he came;
before his feet the clouds were riven,
half darkness and half flame:

But when he came the second time,
he came in power and love;
softer than gale at morning prime
hovered his holy Dove.

There are countless examples one could cite that effectively challenge that simplistic view. In the Hebrew Scriptures, the prophet Elijah famously found God in the 'sound of sheer silence' (1 Kings 19:11-13). Equally, any who want to revel in displays of divine power and wrath are well catered for in the New Testament, not least in the apocalyptic Book of Revelation.

For any who continue to feel that the Old Testament (the Bible Jesus loved) is 'old hat', I hope to suggest otherwise. I shall take some examples from the first two books of the Bible – but examples are exactly what they are, and I hope that this way of reading the texts might then inspire some to look through the same lens at other books in the Hebrew Scriptures. Then I shall move on to consider the specifically Christian Scriptures – 'topping and tailing' the Gospels, so to speak, by focusing on the birth, dying and resurrection of Jesus.

We should not be surprised to find, as we read these extracts through the lens of pastoral companionship, that there are strong resonances between the two sets of ancient writings.

5
Genesis: the book of beginnings

This book – and its opening chapters in particular – may well be among the most ill used in the Bible. The narratives are either dismissed as irrelevant in the post-Enlightenment age or aggressively defended as an alternative science by, respectively, sections of society that appear to be light years apart but are actually closely aligned. Both camps view it from admittedly different theistic standpoints but through the shared lens of literalism! On the basis of literal interpretation of these texts, the most entrenched forms of both atheism and Christianity reach their opposite conclusions and find common ground on which to argue endlessly and equally pointlessly! I hope to approach Genesis rather differently, seeing it as a source not of mere information but of meaningful insight.

For people who view Genesis through the eyes of Jewish or Christian faith, these creation stories hold deep significance. They speak of the direct involvement of God in creation and enable us to relate our search for meaning and purpose to the will and purpose of God. More than that: theists are able to trace back from here to find insights into the nature of God – it would surely be strange if the way God works does not reflect God's nature! None of that is threatened by taking up a different vantage point and examining the text, as we now will, through the lens of the helping relationship. However, hopefully it will also be the case that those whose religious or philosophical outlooks are very different will also find these narratives to be full of powerful insights and wisdom about the human condition.

Fact and truth

Referring to Genesis 1 and 2 as 'creation myths' can easily be misunderstood as suggesting that the chapters are, at best, mistaken nonsense – and that is emphatically not what 'myth' means. Myth is a genre of literature that seeks to explore meaning, to open up mystery – usually with the effect of drawing us in deeper rather than simply clarifying it. It might or might not be based on some factual material – but it is a rich source of *truth* and usually far from nonsense.

For me (irrespective of whether I think they are factual), the opening chapters of Genesis must be read not as creation *accounts* but creation *myths*. They offer us a chance to explore not the 'how' of creation but the 'why' – what does it mean to be part of this immense, mysterious phenomenon? More pertinently for us here: what light can the myths shed upon our role and practice as pastoral companions?

Invitation to become: Genesis 1

This creation narrative is characterised by the call, 'Let there be . . .'. These are the words used to call into being the elements of creation – earth, sky, sea, sun, moon, planets, vegetation and living creatures – filling with vibrant life the empty space that the Creator has made. This has been understood as an imperious command that creation had no option but to obey, but it can be read another way as God creates an ordered space and then invites creation to become, and to fill it.

'The God who lets be' is one of the basic concepts underlying the writing on this subject of John Macquarrie,[25] and that fits very closely with what we see in the unfolding creative process. This is not a carefully supervised process of development but rather a call to free and abundant life. There is little prescription of detail: the Creator simply invites life to flourish. We do not find any scheme imposed on it – elephants here, kangaroos there; creation is simply called to freedom of becoming and appears to be intended to enjoy a huge degree of self-determination.

Indeed, it might be observed that there is a surprising amount of scope for a theory of evolution to coexist with this image, and there are many people of traditional faith who do not have difficulty in accepting evolution as the chosen process for an act of continuous creation in which God is deeply and intimately involved. They would argue that Genesis shows us a process that, far from being in the past, is still ongoing, and will indeed continue for as long as the earth exists.

There is equally powerful imagery here for the process that goes on both within an individual person and within a helping relationship. We do not begin with a preconceived idea of the outcome; rather, we create a therapeutic space and invite life to come forth within it. In the Genesis narrative, this is, of course, a hugely risky approach for the Creator. Clearly there is a very real possibility that the process may run out of control. But then, being 'in control' is something in which God seems less than interested in this narrative. We get the

---

25 Macquarrie, John, *Principles of Christian Theology* (SCM 1979).

impression that the Creator is simply revelling in the new life that is springing up to fill the space created – life which holds the exciting possibility of further and ever-more creative relationship. This God is much more interested in being 'in relationship' than being 'in control'.

Freedom and risk: Genesis 2

Genesis 2, generally considered to be by a different writer (or writers) from Genesis 1, gives us a very different way to understand God as Creator. In this second creation story, the process is much more directive (as well as being in a different sequence), beginning with the creation of a male human and a garden to be his home. In that garden the Creator provides everything the man will need – and something else that is really very odd: the infamous Tree of the Knowledge of Good and Evil. The inclusion of this strange tree raises a fundamental issue about freedom and becoming. One might – indeed should (as I am convinced the writer intended) – ask what God was thinking in planting it and, not content with that, drawing attention to it! This tree brought the possibility – some would say inevitability – of catastrophe to the perfect garden of creation. Why is it there – and why does the writer have God make a point of drawing the man's attention to it?

In the opening part of the chapter, the writer of the story has got into some difficulty. 'How,' the reader will ask, 'did it all go wrong?' How could life in the beautiful garden have changed into the harsh, often brutal struggle for survival that the people of biblical times – in common with countless people today – knew as their reality? Somehow the writer of Genesis has to explain the degeneration that clearly must have happened – and there we have the origin of the myth of the Fall, as an act of wilful disobedience results in banishment from the garden.

But this is more than a literary device. The inspired writer is in fact expressing a very real dilemma presented by our quest for freedom – and known not only to therapists but also to parents, teachers and many others: to allow someone freedom is also to expose them to risk. It might be said that the Creator has no option but to plant that tree and point it out to the occupant of the garden. Without it, what has been created is a gilded cage within which freedom is illusory. The man – and the woman when she is created later – will live out a life of blissful and futile captivity, doing exactly what God has ordained – not as a choice made in free obedience but only because *they do not know how to do otherwise*. The Tree of the Knowledge of Good and Evil is something to which they obviously must have access if they are, in any meaningful sense, to be truly free. But that knowledge – and the power of choice that comes with it – can hardly help but bring the couple unhappiness. Such is the creative dilemma that the writer of Genesis 2 recognises.

This is the anxiety of every therapist and pastoral companion who wants to enable the other to live a free, autonomous life of self-determination. The temptation is to create dependency and keep them close to us. Every ending of therapy is fraught with this anxiety as we fight the temptation to continue the contact for just a little longer. But we are painfully aware of the risks long before that. Sometimes we might reflect that it would be easier to have committed ourselves to a more directive style of counselling. As we seek to empower others to have confidence in their own decisions, we cannot be unaware that they are inevitably going to make some that we will think unwise at the very least. They may even head down a path that we anticipate will lead to unhappiness, regret and possibly disaster. Of course, we can try to make them aware of the risks – as does the Creator in Genesis 2:17:

> 'But of the tree of the knowledge of good and evil you shall not eat, for in the day that you eat of it you shall die.'

Having so warned them, the Creator could no doubt have taken steps to make the tree less accessible, but that does not happen. If the man and woman obey the injunction not to eat it, it must be of their own free choice: that is part of what it means to be human. And when, hardly surprisingly, they do eat from it, they can no longer remain in this state of naive bliss – this gilded cage – but must leave the garden and live in the great, wide, adventurous, dangerous world beyond it. The cost of enabling others to be free, autonomous, fully functioning human beings (a goal, of course, that is never fully attained as the actualising tendency will always seek further development) is that we must live with the expectation that some choices will lead to regrets. The cost of keeping people unfree and dependent (even assuming they would be safer in that state, which is far from certain) would be infinitely higher – for them and for us.

Freedom, failure and responsibility: Genesis 3, 4

Once the possibility of independent decision is known, the elephant is in the room – or, rather, the serpent is in the garden.

> Now the serpent was more crafty than any other wild animal that the Lord God had made.
>
> *Genesis 3:1*

The temptation of Eve by the serpent is an image familiar the world over, whether people have read the Genesis passage or not. This creature voices the temptation that the man and woman would be bound to feel. 'Why would God not want us to eat that fruit? What is wrong with knowing good from evil – surely that's a desirable thing? Knowledge is power – is that what God is afraid of?' Once the fruit is eaten, there is no going back – they cannot unlearn the things they now know, and that means they can never again be happy in the confines of the garden but would destroy it (and probably themselves) in the attempt.

Some people may still remember the World War I song by Joe Young, Sam M. Lewis and Walter Donaldson:

> How ya gonna keep 'em down on the farm
> after they've seen Paree?

It expressed the real and justified anxiety that Americans from rural backgrounds would not be happy returning to their old livelihoods after they had experienced the delights and temptations of Paris during liberation. It had been relatively easy when the old rural life had been all they knew. Now they not only knew about but also had experienced a kind of freedom that had been beyond their power of imagining before. The song predicted that they would never again be happy in the life they had accepted unquestioningly up to that point. But the heart of the dilemma was that they might not be 'happy', in a simple sense of the word, anywhere. Having our horizons opened up can be as costly as it is rewarding.

Carl Rogers faced up to this reality in relation to his own life's work. In a chapter entitled 'A Therapist's View of the Good Life: The Fully Functioning Person', he questioned, on the basis of his research and experience, the view then popular among psychologists that therapy led to happiness *per se*:

> It seems to me that the good life is not any fixed state. It is not, in my estimation, a state of virtue, or contentment, or nirvana, or happiness.[26]

Rather, he proposed:

> The good life is a *process*, not a state of being.
> It is a direction, not a destination.[27]

---

26 Rogers, Carl R., *On Becoming a Person* (Constable 1961, reprinted 2001), pp.185-6.
27 Rogers, *On Becoming a Person*, p.186, original italics.

Later in the chapter, he concluded:

> For me, adjectives such as happy, contented, blissful, enjoyable, do not seem quite appropriate for the process I have called the good life, even though the person in this process would experience each one of those feelings at appropriate times. But the adjectives that seem more generally fitting are adjectives such as enriching, exciting, rewarding, challenging, meaningful.[28]

Rogers was (and indeed still is) considered to be articulating new and challenging insights about the human condition. It has always seemed to me, though, that what he really did was to provide a thorough research base that underpins very ancient wisdom – and for that in itself we owe him a massive debt of gratitude.

This also, incidentally, exposes the fundamental flaw in many popular conceptions of religion: that by committing ourselves to one or other of them we shall achieve a state of happiness. I find this implication in all kinds of places, from papers to pulpits, as people are exhorted to leave behind the illusory pleasures of general society and find 'true happiness' by committing to this or that religion. I suppose it might depend to some extent on how one defines 'happy'. However, the more we learn about the lives of great religious figures, the less convinced we may be that it is an appropriate word to use in any case.

As I read about the lives of the great spiritual pioneers – Moses, Abraham, Jesus, Mohammed, the Buddha – it strikes me increasingly forcefully that their search was much less about the pursuit of happiness and more about meaning and fulfilment. But – and this is a key insight, I think – when faced with the reality that their search for fulfilment was bringing them many things but not what would generally be meant by happiness, all those and many others freely chose to continue the search for fulfilment, even at the risk of their very lives.

So the writers of Genesis – without access to any of the benefits of modern research – have identified the basic dilemma that affects us all: in order to be free, we have to be exposed to risk. We saw this earlier in observing the work of the ape sanctuary, as animals kept (in some cases) as pets were rescued from their gilded cages and exposed to the risks of social living with their own species.

Back in the garden of Eden, the realities of freedom are beginning to make themselves felt. Genesis 3:14-19 portrays life in the wild for the newly released humans. They will find themselves in the real world where they will come into conflict with other species as they compete for food and territory. Instead of simply picking fruit off the trees, they will have to work for their sustenance, and they will

---

28 Rogers, *On Becoming a Person*, pp.195-6.

find that the ground produces not just edible crops but competing weeds that threaten to overrun them. Relationships will change and they will experience pain, sickness and ultimately death.

Those things are often portrayed as punishments for sin, but it is perhaps more accurate – and healthier – to think of them as consequences. It is important not to confuse the two. I remember my son, when he was about 7, experiencing the consequences of a playground accident that had badly damaged one of his teeth. He needed to undergo considerable dental work to repair it. It was essential that the work be done immediately, and he did not understand why further pain had to be heaped upon what he had suffered already. 'But it wasn't my fault!' was the heart-rending cry. We tried, of course, to assure him that he was not being punished, but sometimes painful consequences have to be faced even when we are innocent. His confusion of consequences with punishment is one that is frequently expressed by people many times his tender age.

In eating the fruit, Adam and Eve chose to make the change from being caged pets towards being what Rogers called 'fully functioning persons'. They had become aware of their freedom to 'move in any direction',[29] and that change would have consequences for them: consequences from which even the world's Creator could not protect them – let alone a human therapist or pastoral companion.

Responsibility: Genesis 3, 4

When the writer of Genesis 1 describes the creation of humans, they are said to 'have dominion' over the created order. This word is probably better interpreted as 'wise rule' or 'stewardship'. A more modern (if less attractive) view might be that, having through the evolutionary struggle clawed our way to the top of the food chain and acquired en route the ability to destroy not only other creatures but the very planet itself, we have – like it or not – a responsibility towards the created order. It does not take long for the 'primitive' writers of Genesis to address that issue.

Passing the buck: Genesis 3:12, 13

In microcosm we see a catastrophic breach in relationships, caused in large measure by a failure to accept responsibility and, worse, attempts to shift it to others. The man blames the woman and the

---

29 Rogers, *On Becoming a Person*, p.187.

woman blames the unfortunate animal who has no one left to whom to pass the buck.

Then in Genesis 4 we are told the story of Cain and Abel, the sons of Adam and Eve, who are evidently damaged by the relational difficulties of their parents (the sins of the parents are having consequences for their children – a principle that emerges more explicitly later in the Hebrew Scriptures) and quite unable to live in peace together. In turn, the effect of their broken relationship upon the wider creation is presented to us in chapter 4:10-12:

> [God said] 'Listen; your brother's blood is crying out to me from the ground. And now you are cursed from the ground, which has opened its mouth to receive your brother's blood from your hand. When you till the ground, it will not longer yield to you its strength.'

The key question, though, arose slightly earlier (Genesis 4:9), when God asked Cain, 'Where is your brother?' and received the surly, evasive reply, 'Am I my brother's keeper?' Once again we are back to responsibility.[30]

Many years ago now, at the request of the Church authorities, I did a piece of work in a particular church where there had been problems in relationships with ministers. The process of choosing and calling a minister, in that denomination (as in some others), involved the entire church membership coming to a decision and 'issuing a call'. Usually – maybe after considering a number of possible candidates – the *Church Meeting* will issue a call and the new minister will consider whether to accept. In this particular case, all concerned were anxious that the kind of breakdown in relationships that had previously led to an acrimonious parting should not happen again.

Part of the approach I took was to work with the leadership team and the wider membership around questions of responsibility. The Church Meeting had gone through a process of meeting, hearing and considering the candidate, and the Church Meeting had come to a decision that this person was called by God to be their minister. The minister had likewise met, heard, considered and prayed, and had similarly believed that the call was right. Who, then, carried the responsibility? The answer had to be 'all of us': leadership team, Church Meeting and minister. It was a shared responsibility. If a mistake had been made, it had been a joint one shared by all parties. How, then, would they think fit to approach the matter if disappointment set in later? The answer was, 'Together'. Minister, lay

---

30 I once heard it said that Cain asked the wrong question. His brother had not needed a keeper – he'd needed a brother!

leaders and Church Meeting would all accept shared responsibility rather than scapegoat each other. 'We made a mistake. We have a problem. We need to find a way forward. Together.'

In that way, perhaps, the situation – should it again arise – might be resolved and the pastorate continue or, if it were to seem best to part, that could be accomplished with much less acrimony and pain for all concerned.

We thought earlier about how as pastoral companions or counsellors we are almost destined to disappoint the people with whom we work. However careful the contracting has been, the natural instinct when disappointment sets in is to blame. The pastoral companion must be able to deal with this in a creative way – not dumping the blame (or even part of it) on to the other, and not simply accepting it, either. Indeed, it is important not to use the language of blame at all, but rather to invite the other to reflect on expectations and process. If this is done well, with openness and humility, it is likely that a shared understanding of the process will emerge.

One of the challenges in Family Therapy (a process in which a counsellor will work with a family as a unit in order to resolve difficulties) is to enable people to get past the sticking point where dialogue often ceases. Frequently, the really tough issues are never addressed because each time a conversation reaches that point the family members draw back, fearing conflict, and the dialogue ends or the subject changes. This leaves the unaddressed issue to fester and become even harder to face and, in all probability, blame will be apportioned inappropriately rather than responsibility shared. The family therapist, as a third party, may be the one who is able gently but firmly to keep the dialogue going and to enable the process to continue so that the barrier can be cleared and hitherto unexpressed fears can emerge and be addressed. We are not, of course, working in that area, but it is easy to see how a similar approach in principle might be useful when exploring the disappointment felt by another. In my work with the church mentioned above, there were a number of moments in either church or leadership team meetings when the discussion was in danger of petering out just at the very point that it should most continue. My role was not unlike that of a family therapist in enabling the dialogue to continue and the sticking point to be overcome.

It would be very tempting to continue further in the book of Genesis: the stories of Jacob and Esau, of Joseph and his brothers, and many more would be fascinating to examine through this lens. We have only just scratched the surface, really, and there are great riches to be mined from the rest of it. However, my aim here is not to offer a comprehensive hermeneutic on the entire Bible but rather to illustrate a way of working with it that can be helpful and enlightening, whether or not we come to it from a theistic position.

As far as this current exploration is concerned, I would invite you to join me in examining the Book of Exodus – a particularly rich source of imagery and insights, as well as being a foundational text for both Judaism and Christianity.

6

Exodus: great escapes and epic journeys

The Book of Exodus is, in important ways, the foundational text of the Judaeo-Christian tradition. Literally meaning 'going out', it is about the liberation of the Jewish nation from oppression in Egypt under the pharaohs, and the ensuing journey that led them to what they had come to call the 'Promised Land'. To people of the Jewish and Christian faiths, the book is of monumental importance as the basis of faith in a God who is active in history, working to set people free from oppression and leading them onward to new, fuller life. It provides not only assurance that God cares and keeps promises but also vital insights into what it means to become free and to undertake the inward as well as the outward journey from slavery to freedom – learning, growing, accepting responsibility and facing the demands and conflicts that life in community entails. For the believer, all of that is undertaken under the leadership of the God who goes before and whose promise will not fail. It is probably impossible to overstate its importance to a person of Jewish or Christian faith.

It's not surprising, then, that Exodus has more recently become a particularly rich source of inspiration for the pioneers of theologies of liberation, which embrace the freeing of communities, groups and individuals, of bodies, minds and spirits, seeing those three as inseparable. It was through this lens, before I began my chaplaincy work or trained as a counsellor, that I first came to view Exodus as a treasure-house of learning about the human condition. So it was inevitable that, working in a quasi-counselling environment and then formally training as a counsellor, I would find my experiences frequently driving me back to my religious and spiritual roots – and to this amazing book in particular – as I discovered the powerful resonances that stimulated me to explore further and helped shape my vision of counselling and (as I then called it) pastoral care.

Whether we read it from the perspective of a particular faith tradition or none, the Exodus story gives us some dramatic images of some of the natural processes of life. The word 'journey' is becoming difficult to use because it is so hackneyed, but that does not mean that it is not sometimes the best image – and it is clearly appropriate here. The Exodus is a rich source of inspirational material about the various journeys on which we embark in our lives – some of which we have more choice about than others.

Superficially it is about escaping from slavery to freedom. As we are painfully aware, we easily become enslaved to many things: guilt, grief, regrets, habits, substances, even pleasures that turn out to be fool's gold. The Exodus shows that escape from these is much more likely to be about a long and sometimes tortuous journey than about instant transformation, and a careful reading of it may well make us increasingly suspicious of the quick fix. It has been said that it took God very little time to get the people of Israel out of Egypt, but 40 long years to get Egypt out of Israel.

Exodus is also about learning and growing – something closely associated with escaping from slavery. It was in the desert, as a nomadic race, that the people of Israel learned to leave behind not only the physical but also the mental shackles of slavery and began to grow mentally and spiritually into a nation that could accept stewardship of a country. And it is on similar journeys that we all learn about that process in microcosm as we begin to leave behind the negative attitudes and expectations that were shaped during the time we are calling the past and prepare to be more fully functioning human beings.

My intention here is firmly to resist the temptation (strong as it is) to take Exodus chapter by chapter and end up writing virtually a commentary on it. I think it would be better to focus on a few episodes from the epic journey and see what they can reveal that is helpful in pastoral companionship. In that way I can illustrate the kind of thought process at work, which those who so wish can then apply in a broader reading of the Bible in general.

Regrets, threats and disappointments (Exodus 14)

Having escaped the clutches of Pharaoh, the Israelites are described as 'wandering aimlessly in the land' (verse 3). On a literal level, this is difficult to understand since we have been told as recently as the end of the previous chapter that the guiding pillars of cloud and fire never leave them. However, it is, of course, quite possible to follow 'blindly' where we are led without any sense of aim or purpose.

The story tells how the Egyptian people regret the loss of their slaves and demand that they be caught and returned, upon which Pharaoh sends his army who catch up with the liberated slaves on the shore of the Red Sea. Finding themselves trapped between the advancing army and the expanse of sea, the Israelites blame their leader, Moses, for having got them into that position.

There are four elements in this chapter of Exodus that I should like to highlight and explore: negativity, disappointment, trusting the process, and crossing the sea. Then we shall turn to the later book of Deuteronomy for the end of the Exodus story and consider the issue of letting go.

Negativity: verses 5-9

Clearly, the Egyptians are regretting the liberation of their slaves – and I don't think it's just the fact that they have to do their own washing-up. There would be all kinds of other issues in there around the loss of status, power, control and so on. And on top of all that – well, yes, there was the washing-up. This negativity connects quite vividly with the experience of some people who find that their recovery from illness and dependency is not regarded by others with the undiluted gladness that they might have anticipated. Of these, 'Reg' is a good example.

Reg had a long history of mental health problems and spent regular extended periods of time as an in-patient in mental health units. He had come to regard himself as unable to cope on his own, and had a little network of supportive friends and relatives who fully expected to be part of his life as carers on a more-or-less permanent basis. Most of those people genuinely had his best interests at heart but, as often happens in cases of prolonged mental illness, he also caught the attention of some who sought to exploit his vulnerability. As, against all expectations, Reg began to respond to therapy and develop confidence in making his own decisions, these people felt their positions threatened. To put it bluntly, they had a vested interest in his continuing to be unwell. Gradually, Reg started to reveal in his counselling sessions that he was feeling compromised. His increasing confidence and more assertive behaviour were interpreted by them as signs that he was not well. In his better times he found this ironically amusing since he knew that the real difficulty was precisely the opposite – that he was in a process of recovery and beginning to trust in his own autonomy.

There were, of course, other, more benign reasons for this as well (which undoubtedly were not at play in the Exodus story but are still worth examining here). It can be difficult for those who truly love and care for someone to watch them becoming more independent, simply because (as we saw earlier in 'Watch the monkey' in chapter 1) independence is risky. We learn over time how to help a needy person stay safe within their limitations, but if that person then develops greater autonomy and starts to reassert control over their lives, it can feel very insecure. I recall my family's hoots of amusement when our ageing and infirm mother suddenly expressed her curiosity as to whether she might still be able to ride a bicycle. The hilarity, though, was darkly tinged with anxiety because we knew her well enough not entirely to rule out the possibility that she might actually try to do it! It's an uncomfortable thought, but it would have been understandable for us to feel happier knowing that she was safely confined to a wheelchair.

On a more serious level, that genuine anxiety is very real for carers of vulnerable people such as Reg as they recover. Are they going to overreach themselves and end up worse off than before? Will they become even more vulnerable to those who wish to exploit them? As they strike out more on their own, how will we even be able to monitor their well-being (will they actually manage to stay on the bicycle until they are out of sight before falling off)? All these very legitimate concerns will be there for the true carers as recovery goes on. And, of course, there are the questions which we might find it harder to express but are in fact very natural: 'If my partner becomes more self-confident, will s/he still need me?' 'What is my status in the household/circle of friends, now that I'm not needed for support?' Or it might be simply a feeling that the person we have loved and known is no longer there but has been replaced by someone different. One does not need to be selfish or cynical to experience these anxieties, to which I would argue we are all subject.

Whatever people's motives for involvement, issues like these can affect the socio-psychological environment that is so essential to recovery. Reg found that some of his closest and most trustworthy friends were finding the 'new' Reg difficult to relate to, and in his less-well moments he wondered whether recovery was worth it. The question for his therapist was how to enable him to resist negative pressures without adding to the conflicts or, heaven forbid, actually becoming involved in them as a third party. We shall come to that in a moment, but if we take the Exodus passage in sequence, we now observe a different but related phenomenon.

Disappointment: verses 10-14

By way of making Moses' position even worse – if that were possible – the Israelites whom he is attempting to liberate now round on him and blame him for their situation. It is he, after all, who has led them out of slavery in the first place (as if they had no option but to follow . . .). And it really hasn't worked out the way they were hoping. Far from being instantly whisked away to a life of blissful freedom, they have found themselves in a different captivity – surrounded by hostile, infertile desert and caught up in an arduous journey that they don't understand.

Perhaps it is at this point that they realise the uncertainty of their position and their unpreparedness for it. Well, it has to be somebody's fault, and the only (or certainly the most obvious) candidate for that is the person who, as they now see it, dragged them out there. So they round on Moses, accusing him of bringing them there to die, which of course now makes 'serving the Egyptians' a less unattractive prospect (it is significant how their slavery has by now changed in their perceptions to 'service' – a position of much greater dignity). Clearly, this is a case of distance lending enchantment to the view – distance allied to the heavily tinted lenses of their present experience. This is a classic example of the disappointment referred to earlier (see chapter 2, 'Qualities of presence'). In Reg's case, as it happens, he did not express disappointment in his therapist. Indeed, it was remarkable that in years of quite intensive work he never did so. Some other clients naturally and understandably did, however, and inevitably a few sadly took the option to return to their 'Egypt' rather than continue the journey, leaving me to process my own disappointment and the feelings that went with it.

The challenge that this presents to a therapist or pastoral companion is something we looked at earlier, where I observed that the important thing for the therapist/companion is to trust the process and resist the pressure to 'do something' to save face or to offer short-term comfort to the other (something we shall return to again in considering the suffering and dying of Jesus). And that is the course of action that Moses took, but I have a feeling it was not as straightforward as it might appear.

Trusting the process: verses 15-29

As the Egyptian armies bear down upon them, spreading understandable panic among the Israelites which the latter then experience and express as anger, it is not hard to imagine Moses feeling almost intolerable pressure to do something – and to do it quickly. To me, two possible options present themselves.

Moses might decide that the wise and responsible action would be to admit that the experiment has failed. At this point it should be possible to negotiate the people's safety. As they themselves have expressed, 'serving the Egyptians' would at least mean they keep their lives in the short term. It might provide breathing space to think of a better strategy and find another route. The clear intention of the Egyptians is to recapture the slaves, not to kill them, and even if some are killed as an example, surrendering would offer a good chance of saving the lives of the rest and limiting the damage. Yes, perhaps some skilful negotiation – by a man who had, after all, been part of Pharaoh's household – might be the best option.

The other option – less credible, but then people do some truly incredible things under less pressure than this – would be to rally the people's spirits and make some kind of stand. It's not hard to imagine that the outcome, in purely human terms, would be tragic, but it's an option all the same.

Faced with these choices, Moses takes neither of them, but stands firm against the pressure from the people and calls upon them to trust God. I am not going to suggest that such glib advice would be appropriate to a vulnerable person feeling threatened by the very process that was expected to make things better. What is happening here is a little more complex than that.

The biggest challenge to Moses is not the sea, or the advancing forces of oppression, but the internal turmoil in the minds of the people. The immediate need is that they stay committed to their journey rather than being panicked into an unhelpful reaction. And the role of Moses here is critical – quite literally standing firm under the most appalling pressure from all sides while awaiting the unfolding of the process. The popular misconception is that Moses reaches out his staff and the waters immediately part – but reading the text carefully shows that that is not how it happens. There is a long night's waiting ahead, during all of which he is doubtless still being harangued for his grandiose incompetence and everything in him – as well as everyone around – cries out to him, 'Don't just stand there – *do something!*'

That may be the role of the pastoral companion when the other is feeling disappointed, discouraged or pressurised not to continue the process. Moses says, 'Stand firm and trust God.' One of my counselling tutors would have said, 'Stand firm and trust the process.'

In my work with Reg, it might then be said that I had three lines of approach to the issue:

- As a person of faith, I was called to trust God.
- As a counsellor working within a secular system, I was called to trust the process.
- As a person of incarnational faith (more on which later), I was called to trust that God was *in* the process.

The common factor in all of this was that I had to stand firm – and enable Reg to do the same.

The temptations were huge – there were ways I might perhaps become more involved. I could meet with Reg's family to try to reassure them – perhaps bring them a little more on side (after all, we all wanted the same thing in the end). I knew, though, that that would be fraught with perils, not for me so much as for Reg, and would certainly compromise my role as his counsellor. It might, though, have been less catastrophic than the other temptation which sometimes was inexpressibly hard to resist: to wade into the fray in defence of Reg against those other people who were clearly exploiting his vulnerability and had reason to obstruct his recovery. Clearly, I could not do either – not least because I would undermine completely the self-confidence Reg was painfully building up, but also because I had neither the qualifications nor the remit to function either as a family therapist (a specific specialism in counselling) or as a knight in shining armour. And there was also the little matter of professional conduct!

It was not comfortable to stand on the shores of this 'Red Sea' for what turned into a very long 'night', while all around and within me the voices screamed for action, and my own inner dialogue centred upon my pathetic powerlessness in the situation.

In all this, both Reg and I, to different extents, were learning what it meant for me not to be the rescuer that he and many others had expected me to be (and that I sometimes felt impelled to become). If people need rescuing then that has to be done by others with the training, facilities and, not least, the authority to do it. Our role is to stand firm – and to enable the other to do the same.

That is, until the waters part – and then it is something else entirely.

Crossing the sea: verses 21-25

After the long wait, we read that Moses' faith and determination pay off and the miracle happens as the waters of the sea part, leaving a path of dry land along which the Israelites can escape from the Egyptian army. It sounds simple enough – but perhaps we might make the effort to imagine the feelings of people stepping onto that path and undertaking a long journey between the walls of water held apart by nothing more concrete than the wind!

A long-term service user and counselling client, 'Eleanor', had experienced a crushing personal tragedy and had quite simply been unable to deal with it. For two long years she had lived in denial, and the effect of this on her own and her family's well-being would fill a book in itself. When she came to me she was desperate as the grief had caught up with her and made clear that this time it was not to be fobbed off but had to be taken seriously.

Denial is one of the classic stages of the grieving process, which probably all people experience to some extent and generally work their way through in due course. It might well be said that it is, indeed, an essential part of our coping system as the brain admits the experience to our awareness gradually, as we are able to handle it. Occasionally someone will become 'stuck' in the process and may need some help to recommence the journey. That also is not particularly unusual.

Eleanor was different in that she was stuck at the very *beginning* of the journey. From quite early childhood, she had been schooled in what I can only describe as a particularly extreme stoicism, and had been conditioned to suppress rather than express feelings that were considered negative. So what was she to do when suddenly and traumatically faced with the worst kind of bereavement, but deny it? By the time she came to me, after two years of determined and emotionally exhausting denial, she was not surprisingly at the end of her tether. She had realised that there was to be no peace for her unless she could stop the grief from getting to her; and that was becoming manifestly impossible as it was determinedly kicking down the door of her awareness and demanding admission. After a number of attempts to end her life, she decided in desperation to seek help in order to live it.

Like the Israelites at the Red Sea, Eleanor felt she could not escape the monster that was pursuing her. The only way forward, she realised, was to make the terrible journey that she had been refusing to make and go through the grief process – beginning by admitting to her awareness the reality of the bereavement. However, that thought in itself terrified her, as all her childhood conditioning admonished her that grief was dangerous and would destroy her if she gave it the opportunity.

Her psychological position was strikingly similar to that of the Israelite slaves, fleeing from tyranny and now finding themselves trapped – in a horribly real sense, as the proverb says – 'between the devil and the deep blue sea'. It may well be that Eleanor came for therapy in the hope that there was a third way – or that I would have some wise advice that would take the threat away. But all I could offer was to be a companion as she made the journey of her life.

As we worked together and trust began to be established, I broached very tentatively the subject of Bible narratives – Eleanor had a deep-seated aversion to religion, having been exposed to a very unhealthy form of it earlier in life – and then asked her to consider the feelings of the Israelites. She recognised the parallel immediately, and we imagined together what the journey would have been like: the initial moment of commitment as they stepped from shore to seabed; hearing the roar of the wind and the waters and sensing the inexpressible danger of the situation; the ground sloping down as they moved deeper into the sea and the water became higher, the noise louder, the threat greater; then the ground flattening out and beginning to rise – a sign of the start of the outward journey and the beginning of hope with the prospect of land – and finally the emergence from the sea to the safety of dry land in a different place. Needless to say, we did not go into the negative aspects of the storytelling – why, for example, the storytellers chose to take such delight in drowning the Egyptians – but focused on the specific images that I was hoping would be helpful.

Eleanor caught the imaginative process immediately, and returned to it frequently during later counselling sessions. She would speak of how the 'ground under her feet' felt – whether it was still sloping downward, had levelled out or had turned upward as she began to emerge from between the threatening walls of water.

It took five seemingly interminable years for her to cross her 'Red Sea' – five years of trauma and genuine danger that she had never thought she could face and survive. At times in the earlier stages there seemed a real threat that the waters would return and swamp her, and at those times we would talk about her options. Sometimes she was tempted to go back, but she knew there was nothing desirable back there for her, and in any case she did not want to waste the pain she had gone through to get thus far. Her only viable option at this stage was to 'trust the process'. Then the time came when she sensed the ground beginning to slope upward and began to feel she was on the exit side of the process. The terrifying journey was far from over, but gradually her confidence grew that we were on the way to new life.

As I write this, years after the end of Eleanor's therapy, her situation is dramatically different. The psychological scars from her past remain, and sometimes make themselves felt, but the wounds are no longer open. She goes through dark times still, especially in dealing with further bereavements, but this time she knows from experience that the process is not life threatening and that she can make the (now much less dramatic) journey in confidence. Indeed, during the 'Red Sea' stage of her therapy, she underwent further bereavements, and it was heartening to see her incorporate the fresh grief into her journey.

Eleanor's was a particularly dramatic example arising in a very specialised area, and the work was done in the context of a mutually supportive multidisciplinary team and under rigorous clinical supervision. Pastoral companions and ministers may hope not to become involved in cases quite as complex or threatening as hers, and if they feel called to do so, should only agree when satisfied that the necessary skills as well as robust support systems are in place. More probably, they would seek to refer on to a specialist service, of which I shall say more in the final chapter. However, there will be many less-complex cases – including (but not only) more usual bereavements – where people need help and support to embark on a difficult journey. Eleanor's story, and her healing, gives some insight into the power of Scripture – and, indeed, of story generally – when used creatively, even for people who do not 'buy the package' in theistic terms.

I would say that in some way or other we all have our own 'Red Sea experiences'. One such for me was my first-ever need for invasive surgery, which came much later than for many people, in my retirement. It was fortunately a minor operation with few risks, but there are always risks with any such intervention – and the fact that the condition was not life threatening made the decisive step harder to take. I faced not one but several 'Red Sea moments':

- Taking the decision to consult my GP about symptoms.
- Attending out-patients appointments.
- Not least, actually showing up at the hospital on the day of the operation.
- Finally, allowing the anaesthetist to put me under, knowing that from then onward I really was irrevocably committed and had to trust not only the process but also other people.

Like Eleanor (although my circumstances were otherwise not remotely to be compared with hers), I was feeling that I could not continue living with the increasingly uncomfortable symptoms, and so the only way to go was forward – but knowing that did not make it easy.

I have taken just a few highlights of the Exodus tradition as examples of looking at Scripture through the eyes of a pastoral companion or counsellor. I end this exposition with something not from the Book of Exodus itself, but clearly from the Exodus *tradition*, which is perhaps one of the most important – and difficult – lessons anyone involved in pastoral companionship has to learn.

Letting go: Deuteronomy 34:1-8

This story of the death of Moses might seem a strange one to include – hopefully we do not need to prepare every person for the possible death of their pastoral companion. However, this is really about endings generally – and in particular the untimeliness of them.

Any period of pastoral companionship has to have an ending. I'm not thinking here of the system of general pastoral oversight used in many churches where everyone on the leadership team – elder, deacon or whatever – has a list of church people towards whom they have an ongoing pastoral responsibility; clearly that is an open-ended relationship of a very general nature. Rather I am thinking of the specific, focused involvement of a pastoral companion with another who is experiencing a time of particular need.

Reading this passage from Deuteronomy, we might think the writer is portraying God in a poor light as Moses is taken tantalisingly to the mountain-top, shown all the land that the people will occupy, and then told that he won't be alive to go there with them. However, that is surely one of the realities of life and death – of beginnings and endings – with which we are all too familiar. Parents look forward to seeing their children grow up; and when they do and all seems accomplished, along come the grandchildren, awakening fresh hopes and dreams. Some grandparents see their grandchildren grow up, too – and then along come great-grandchildren . . . Sooner or later we all have to face the reality that we shall not see our hopes and dreams fulfilled.

This is also, of course, something that was very real for me during my time in teaching – and for all of my colleagues, too. Every year would see mass endings as an entire intake from years earlier crossed over into a new world of work, university or whatever. Many of them had given us the privilege of accompanying them on important journeys that shared some of the characteristics of Exodus. A few would perhaps stay in touch for a while, but we knew it was an ending and there was no way we could be part of the exciting and perilous new life that we had helped them to find. For some we had high hopes; for others, anxieties; and for many, both to some degree. But we were all obliged, to paraphrase the old spiritual, to 'let the people go'.

In many aspects of experience, there will always be endings – cruel separations from things it would have been nice for us to be around to see, but at some stage that hope will be frustrated. What we might well learn from this is that seeing the outcome of our endeavours is not something we can always expect in this world.

The great iconic liberator, Martin Luther King Jnr, referred to this Deuteronomy passage in his famous 'mountain-top' speech the night before his assassination:

> Like anybody, I would like to live a long life. Longevity has its place. But I'm not concerned about that now. I just want to do God's will. And he's allowed me to go up to the mountain. And I've looked over. And I've seen the Promised Land. I may not get there with you. But I want you to know tonight, that we, as a people, will get to the promised land!

And so I'm happy, tonight.
I'm not worried about anything.
I'm not fearing any man!
Mine eyes have seen the glory of the coming of the Lord![31]

Doubtless it is already becoming clear that there are real connections here with pastoral companionship.

One of the roles of a pastoral companion, as we have observed already, is to be a witness to hope, to keep the vision alive for someone whose life is at such a low ebb that they cannot see it. When I was working with Eleanor, it was important to witness to hope when all she could see was the water threatening to overwhelm her. However, there will come a time when the companionship has to end, and the vital element then is that the companion must not have become so addicted to the vision as to want to claim a piece of the action.

This is perhaps the most difficult thing for anyone involved in people-centred work to learn. All too easily, caring can turn to dependence, not only on the part of the other but of the companion as well. The satisfaction and sometimes sheer joy of seeing the other begin to experience new life can be addictive. And, we might argue, what is unnatural about wanting to be part of the renewal, especially when we have probably shared some dark and scary times along the way? Surely we have earned it?

Here we return to the matter of respecting the otherness of the other. As a companion I am not involved in that relationship for what I can get out of it. That I do derive something from it (perhaps in terms of personal and professional satisfaction, and my own learning and development) is a truth it would be unhealthy to deny – but that is not my reason for being there.

I recall how one of my early counselling clients began by telling me why she had not continued with a previous counsellor. The person had developed a dependency on the client and clearly wanted the mutuality of friendship rather than the asymmetrical relationship of companion and other. When the client decided to end the therapy, the counsellor became openly needy and petulantly asked, 'So what about me?'

That was an unusual case, but all of us involved in pastoral work or counselling know the sense of bereavement that can come with letting go, especially when the work has been prolonged and in depth. There are two issues that are particularly significant here.

---

31 From the speech by Martin Luther King Jnr on 3 April 1968, the day before his assassination, at the Mason Temple (Church of God in Christ) Headquarters in Memphis, Tennessee.

Whose life is it anyway?

The first issue is very clear: as expressed above, we are here for the others; not they for us. In a counselling context this will usually mean a complete ending at an agreed appropriate time with no further contact beyond that.[32] This is prepared for as part of the work, and the awareness will have been there from the beginning. It has been well said that all bereavement counselling is preparation for its ending. One of the key things we are trying to achieve is to enable others to live autonomous lives, to be confident in their own decision-making, to trust their own instincts, and so on. This will be defeated if we feel we can never let go – and indeed that would certainly say more about our own neediness than that of the other.

When Moses sees the Promised Land from the mountain-top, he would be less than human if he does not experience, with all the joy, some qualms of anxiety. Are the people really ready for all that responsibility? What if they get it horribly wrong (as, of course, we now know they did) and throw away all 'his' good work? What a waste the 40-year endurance mission would then have been! Surely he cannot be expected to put all his investment in the people at risk. However, Moses is not given the option. His role, once again, is to trust God; to trust the process that has gone before; and to believe that among the people's accomplishments is also the resilience, resourcefulness and indeed wisdom to find their own way, make their own mistakes and face the inevitable 'wilderness' experiences of the future with faith and commitment.

It is a hard calling, indeed, to be the one who has the vision, to be part of the journey towards its fulfilment, and then, at the most exciting moment, to be denied – or to know one must deny oneself – the joy of its final fulfilment.

But what does 'final fulfilment' mean? That is the second issue.

Chasing perfection

During my work with Eleanor, I was acutely aware of this. After all that we had gone through together, the idea (however unlikely) that she might at the last stage regress and throw it all away was unbearable, and the prospect of ending might just possibly have been almost as threatening to me as to her – I certainly struggled hard with

---

32 The reader will have picked up that I am clearly still in touch with one or two of the 'others' from my working life. This is why I said 'usually'. Of the hundreds of others with whom I worked over four decades, there are just four with whom I am still in touch on a very sporadic, occasional basis – statistically, one for every ten years!

the idea not only before but after the end of therapy. I reflected on the issues, not infrequently, with my clinical supervisor who helped keep two important and fundamental questions before me.

First of all, she asked, did I truly trust the process that Eleanor and I had been through? Had we reached the point where *irreversible* change had taken place? Undoubtedly, Eleanor would experience hard times and make mistakes, but I knew, even without the reminder, that I could not prevent that anyway. Apart from anything else, being her infallible source of wisdom had never been part of my role. I also knew that I had no real option in the matter because the one thing most guaranteed to undo our good work together, and to turn my anxiety into self-fulfilling prophecy, was for me neurotically – and narcissistically – to cling on to her.

Perhaps the most illuminating question my supervisor asked, however, was her second one: 'When will you feel your work is done? When she hasn't cried for a month? When she gets a job? When she turns into Supermum, and her dysfunctional family into a shining example of domestic bliss and harmony? Just what kind of idyllic perfection are you hoping for?'

Of course, we both knew the answer. The question was not, 'Is everything now perfect for Eleanor?' Things would never be perfect for Eleanor any more than they are for the rest of us. The question was, 'Is it time for *her* to take possession of *her* promised land?' The time when that would be the next step came closer and closer. Despite all my anxieties, I wanted to see it happen, as did she.

No, I was not Moses, or Martin Luther King Jnr – my mountain-top was rather lower and my vision more limited – but I had been there and seen it, and I knew that if Eleanor was ever to live the new life she had risked so much to find, it had to be without me.

7

The birth narratives of Jesus

We have had just a taster of the wealth of imagery and wisdom available in the Hebrew Scriptures – also known as the Old Testament. I would encourage further exploration, looking at other books in that canon through the lens we have created, but space prohibits that we do it here.

So I propose now to move on to the specifically Christian Scriptures (the 'New Testament') and focus upon the Gospels, which set out in narrative form the life and ministry of Jesus as interpreted by the evangelists. There are powerful insights to be found all through these books – and, indeed, the rest of the Christian Scriptures – but they are particularly striking in the areas on which I propose to focus: the birth of Jesus, his dying and his resurrection, which we shall consider later.

All of these areas bring out a particular aspect of distinctively Christian spirituality – something that is certainly not completely absent from other faiths but which I personally have only found accorded this kind of centrality in the Christian tradition: the Incarnation.

It is difficult to know the exact process by which the beliefs about Jesus came about, but it is not unlikely that it happened something like this. During what we now think of as the first half-century of the Common Era, an itinerant Jewish preacher by the name of Yeshua – Jesus – was developing something of a following in the Roman province of Judaea. He stood out as different from the establishment figures in a number of ways, perhaps most of all for his scandalous disregard for the social mores of his time. In a lifestyle characterised by compassion, he touched people who were considered to be ritually impure; he not only entered the homes of social outcasts but also actually shared table fellowship with them (a clear sign of acceptance and friendship in that culture). In general, he seemed to value most highly those whom society ignored or despised. He built up a following of people who eventually (at what precise time is not clear) became convinced that in him they had encountered the very heart of God; a God radically different from the one beloved of the establishment who was, by way of contrast, legalistic, judgemental, deeply exclusive and very much on the side of the privileged and the conventional.

Understandably, this challenge alarmed and angered those who represented the official religion, and the outcome was that Jesus died a horrible death, held up to ridicule as a powerless pretender. This action, designed to destroy any credibility he might have had, backfired badly, and instead his death came to set the seal on his life as a new revelation of God: God whose defining qualities were compassion and humility; whose power was the transforming potential of love – love that renounced coercive power in favour of relationship and was prepared to suffer rejection and any amount of pain for the sake of the other. However, this was not an impotent, wimpish deity, but one who *chose*, at any cost, to invest everything in the power of love to transform and renew. The power and the glory of this God were of a different order completely.

Within a short time of Jesus' death, not only had that event been reinterpreted as a victory, but also his followers were claiming to have experienced his presence in ways that could only be described in terms of resurrection. The key aspect for our purposes, though, is the re-envisioning of the God-concept in terms of power-renunciation, relationship and suffering love. I suppose we might say that the idea was as revolutionary – and for many incomprehensible – in the first century CE as was the concept of 'non-directive counselling' in the twentieth! It is not difficult to see that the kind of spirituality that would grow up around such a re-envisioning might offer some helpful insights and images for our way of being with one another, and for the concept of the healing power of presence.

I propose to begin with the birth narrative in the opening chapters of the Gospel according to Luke. This is well known to most people as part of the Christmas story when Christians celebrate the birth of God as a vulnerable human baby in a place of poverty represented by the placing of the baby in a manger for a crib, there being 'no room at the inn'.

Taken seriously, the concept of Incarnation has the power to revolutionise our understanding about the nature of humanity and the relationships between the human and the divine. And if that does not shape and transform our practice in pastoral ministry, then I really am at a loss to know what will. But for that to happen we have to get rather beyond the sentimentality of the popular Christmas crib scene and engage seriously with the question of the relationship between divinity and humanity, which is what that story is intended to enable. A key statement about this relationship was made by one of the early Church Fathers:

> The glory of God is [humanity] fully alive, and to be alive consists in beholding God.[33]

Whether one is a Christian believer within the mainstream tradition, a non-theist seeking to find meaningful spirituality in the ancient

---

33 St Irenaeus (second-century Bishop of Lyon), *Against Heresies, Book 4*, 20:7 c185 CE.

writings, or at some point between, this statement is little-short of mind-blowing. In summary, it means that we find supreme beauty, the fulfilment of our highest aspirations, the highest of values – the meaning of life, no less – not somewhere outside our world or universe, and not in the more obvious icons within it, but in the life-fullness of a human being or of humanity. This idea is utterly contrary to popular ideas of divinity that see it as the polar opposite of humanity and the two as irreconcilable. The Christian doctrine of the Incarnation – of God becoming human – calls us instead to find the divine within humanity. And Irenaeus says that when human beings experience life in its fullness, then we see the true glory of God – and when we see that glory we ourselves experience the fullness of life. If that sounds like a circular argument, that is because it is. Or rather, it's a double spiral: outward, leading to ever-greater experience of life and of God; and inward as it takes us deeper into ourselves and our own spiritual life and God at its epicentre.

Perhaps I might take a few moments to illustrate that idea first, and then we shall use the birth narratives from the Gospels to shed further light on it.

I worked with 'Marion' for a year or so. For a good part of that time she would adopt a protective position on a chair, her feet drawn up on the seat as she huddled into the back as if trying to stay as far away as possible, her arms crossed in front of her holding her rolled-up coat as a barrier, while her fingers nervously unravelled, twisted and generally rendered unusable my supply of paper clips. This last exercise seemed in some way to facilitate her process so after a few sessions I took to ensuring there were some close to hand wherever we were to meet. It seemed pretty obvious to me that she found my presence scary – and there might have been various reasons for that, not entirely (though quite possibly partly) to do with my height, weight or (usually controlled) tendency to be overbearing. However, she assured me that her posture was (psychologically) for my protection, not hers, representing her deep-seated fear that what she felt was destroying her from inside would be dangerous for me, too. Over a period of time, as the core conditions took effect, she began to unfold herself into a more unremarkable posture until the coat could be set aside completely and she jokingly assured me that the paper clips were safe.

Our work together ended when Marion started a new life in a different part of the country, but I knew little more than that. A couple of years later we encountered one another by chance at an unrelated social event. She looked at me for a moment and said, 'I'm sorry, but I'm going to hug you.'

As she did so, I asked, 'Why "sorry"?'

'Well,' she smiled, 'I'm probably breaking some boundary or other!'

That hug, later followed by an invitation to her wedding – which was a wonderful day full of love, laughter, joy and most of all life – caught the flavour of Irenaeus' words: 'the glory of God is [humanity] fully alive'. It had been among the most inexpressible privileges of my life to be present, week by week, as she began to find the glory of God within herself. No matter how many times I witnessed that over my career, with a wide variety of people, it never lost its power to enthral and inspire me. I have often described the general process as watching, on a slow-motion video, a flower opening to the sun – slowly releasing the petals from their protective huddle and letting in the light to reveal, at first tentatively but then ever more confidently, the glory within.

To find the divine glory in a human personality should not, of course, seem particularly startling if we take seriously the claim made in the very first chapter of the Bible:

> Then God said, 'Let us make humankind *in our image, according to our likeness.'*
>
> *Genesis 1:26 (my emphasis)*

Christian Scriptures and tradition claim nothing less than that God was made most visible when revealed in flesh-and-blood humanity in all the vulnerability of a baby (and, as we shall later see, in the agony of death by crucifixion). On top of that, countless people down the ages have come to find in those images a kind of power and glory beyond anything to be found in a palace. For what it is worth, I have had the privilege of visiting a palace – as an invited guest at a Buckingham Palace garden party – and I'm confident that none of its usual residents would feel offended by my categorically saying that I wholeheartedly agree: there is no glory, no beauty, no splendour that I have either experienced or imagined anywhere that remotely begins to come close to what I have witnessed in a therapy room.

I have also learned to value the second half of Irenaeus' maxim: 'To be alive consists in beholding God.' Although I am wary of using the word 'mutuality' in a counselling or pastoral companionship context as it can hold serious dangers, I have to say that it is there to a certain degree in the process I have described. As I witness the glory of God in humanity fully alive, I also experience life within myself in more vibrant and fulfilling ways. This, of course, does not have to be in the pastoral companionship or therapy context: we find it also in our other social interactions. However, without detracting from the beauty of the flower fully open to the sun, there is something special beyond words about witnessing the opening process itself.

Bringing hope to birth

The gospel does not say simply that God came to earth and chose to live in a place of poverty and oppression. That in itself would certainly be an inspiring idea – but it says more than that. It says that God was *brought to birth* in such a place. I have found the birthing image a powerful one as, out of pain and risk, new life, with all its attendant hope and joy, emerges into the world.

Rogers himself used the analogy powerfully in the preface to his book, *Client-Centred Therapy*, as he felt around for a definition of what the book was about. He said that as well as being about the client:

> It is about me as I rejoice at the privilege of being midwife to a new personality – as I stand by with awe at the emergence of a self, a person, as I see a birth process in which I have had an important and facilitating part. It is about both the client and me as we regard with wonder the potent and orderly forces which are evident in the whole experience, forces which seem deeply rooted in the universe as a whole.[34]

To talk about the birth of a new personality may perhaps seem to be over-egging the pudding a little in terms of general pastoral companionship – although it is certainly utterly appropriate, and indeed powerfully evocative, in relation to in-depth therapy with profoundly damaged people. Yet while most of us may not be privileged to witness transformation of the kind Rogers saw, it is far from unusual for long-suppressed *aspects* of personality to emerge as the core conditions enable the other to acknowledge these aspects. In terms of the feelings this evokes in the companion or therapist, that of witnessing birth is probably the closest description available: we may have been with the other through difficult and even scary times as they struggled to release whatever was within them, and the best reward possible is to see the outcome and share the joy from all that. Such moments have been among the most privileged I can remember.

There is, though, something far more profound here for the Christian believer. Jesus taught us to seek God in humanity. Might it be possible that what is emerging when we are with an other is not only, as Rogers says, the emergence of a human self but the manifestation of the divine within the human? As in Bethlehem, so in countless other places and circumstances in the world, people struggle with pain and risk to bring to birth a vision of God incarnate.

---

34   Rogers, Carl R., *Client-Centred Therapy* (Constable 1965, reprinted 2001), p.x-xi.

The birthing image has always seemed particularly evocative in terms of the role of women in liberation movements (and as we saw when considering Exodus, pastoral companionship can be in large measure about liberation). In Apartheid South Africa, for example, women in townships and shanties engaged in a painful and dangerous struggle to bring to birth, and nurture – at once literally and metaphorically – the hope of the nation. Sometimes that was literally about children, but it was also about many other things as they daily faced the challenge of not only living in those places but also creating and sustaining hope within them.

This was, of course, not unique to the African continent. I recall a conversation in a house on the Shankhill Road in Belfast, during the terrible period known with classic understatement as 'the Troubles' before the signing in 1998 of the Good Friday agreement. Images from Northern Ireland of bombed-out buildings and disfigured or frightened people had for three decades been regular fare on the news media, and many of us would have felt (perhaps with a tinge of shame) glad that we were not living in that place. The Falls and Shankhill Road were familiar to us as, respectively, Republican and Unionist heartlands, each a virtual no-go area for the other.

I was introduced to a family on the Shankhill Road who offered me tea and home-made cake using a beautiful bone-china tea service. As we talked, I felt how incongruous it all seemed. I could have been in almost any comfortable middle-class home in mainland Britain, but the conversation would have been very different. In a remarkably matter-of-fact way, the family talked about their experiences of life in their city of fear. They spoke of a local pub that had been bombed a number of times, and doubtless would be again. And when it was, the local people would again turn out to claw away the rubble and pull people out until the emergency services arrived to take over.

I had to ask the obvious question: 'Why do you stay here?' One thing that was clear was that this particular couple were relatively well fixed financially and could surely – considering that their very survival might depend on it – have extricated themselves.

Their reply was as breathtaking as it was unassuming: 'We have to stay here. There is a need for us here. We cannot abandon this place, and with it others who have no option but to stay.'

That very ordinary-seeming retired couple had made a conscious choice to remain in that place, with all the risks, as a sign of hope for others. They were the living, breathing evidence that God had not abandoned inner-city Belfast but was alive and well in human flesh and blood – and there was plenty of the latter – as well as in the townships of South Africa, the *favelas* of Latin America, not to mention many grim, hard-faced places in the part of the world that calls itself 'developed'. This was incarnational theology in action – at great personal cost.

It may seem a grandiose claim, but this – on a smaller and more personal scale – is what we choose to do when we enter into someone else's frame of reference as a pastoral companion. On the purely human level, we become a sign of hope: someone cares enough to do this, which says that there is goodness in the world and that just possibly there may be hope, whatever contrary evidence the other party experiences in their situation. More than that, though, it carries the message that they are of value. If a person with no need to do so will not only spend time with me but actually *choose* to do so in a difficult and possibly scary emotional place, then it at least begins to suggest that I am of value and, perhaps in some sense or other, even lovable.

For a Christian believer, it says much, much more. Could it be that God – God who chooses to be known and experienced in human flesh and blood – is in this with me after all? Am I seeing in this caring presence a glimpse of incarnate God?

There is, however, an inherent danger in considering this latter example – that we simplistically identify the divine presence with the 'companion' role. I have already mentioned examples where the divine glory has been made visible to me in the other. Irenaeus' maxim should always point us towards this corrective: as pastoral companions we should be alert to signs of 'the glory of God in [the other] fully alive'.

The hope is within us

An appropriate extension of this line of thought is the principle of hope and healing emerging from within, rather than being imported from outside the situation. In the Christmas story, the Redeemer in whom the hope of wholeness (not only of a nation but of the world) is invested is born and grows *within the situation*. In a pastoral encounter, the hope and power for change lies not in the pastoral companion or counsellor but *within the other* – in the person who is needing and seeking help. The role of the companion is not, in classic B-movie terms, to be the US 9th Calvary riding over the hill to rescue the trapped and helpless victim. We are there to be facilitators of a process that will take place within the other. It will often involve struggle, pain and even risk, and the role of the pastoral companion is to facilitate the birth.

Rogers described a number of learning encounters that shaped his understanding of counselling, and one particular lights-on moment that crystallised a fundamental insight:

This incident was one of a number which helped me to experience the fact – only fully realised later – that it is the client who knows what hurts, what directions to go, what problems are crucial, what experiences have been deeply buried. It began to occur to me that unless I had a need to demonstrate my own cleverness and learning I would do better to rely upon the client for the direction of movement in the process.[35]

What this amounts to is that the resources for change, for liberation and for wholeness are already there within the other. Our role is to facilitate the birth that will bring them into the light of day and make them more readily available to the other. This will be about the core conditions and the power of presence, and not about the exercise of expertise or our own power.

Relationship, power and empowerment

At the heart of the person-centred approach to counselling is the renunciation of power for the sake of relationship. Something I have learned over many years – and something that I now find at the heart of the Christian faith – is that we cannot have a meaningful and satisfying relationship with another at the same time as exercising power over them (however good our motives may appear). This, we remember, was God's dilemma as Creator in Genesis. The more we want relationship, the more we have to relinquish power, to acknowledge their otherness – 'to look the other honestly in the face [and] recognise someone I cannot control'.

Relationship is at the heart of pastoral companionship and of counselling. As has been mentioned before, it is becoming increasingly evident that the vital factor in therapy is the relationship between therapist and client – between pastoral companion and other. The first requirement is that the counsellor or pastoral companion renounces any desire to control or manipulate the other. This is incredibly difficult to do. Indeed, it can be said that it is impossible to eradicate completely the power of the therapist. The mere fact that one person who is in need has come to another because they feel they might be able to help – that alone carries not only the perception but also the reality of power, and it is vital that the companion is realistic about this and in a state of sufficient congruence to deal with it.

---

35 Rogers, *On Becoming a Person*, pp.11-12.

According to Christian tradition – and Luke's infancy narrative in particular – God's way of dealing with this was to come into our lives in the most vulnerable form imaginable: a newborn baby. The image has its limitations, of course, as will be immediately apparent. It is emphatically not to be recommended, for example, that companions and counsellors make themselves dependent upon the others (although vulnerability is in a different sense certainly involved). However, perhaps extreme measures are required for God! It does not take much imagination to see that for the almighty Creator of all things to come and inhabit the same room would present huge difficulties in relating in a power-free way: 'Just forget that I'm God and behave normally!'

So this might be said to be an extreme case, but it does illustrate well the renunciation of power and the difficulties, as well as opportunities, that that can present.

We have observed before that to be in someone else's life while totally respecting their 'otherness' is to relinquish control, and that feels extremely vulnerable. The God who chooses to relinquish all power and security in order to be present to the world is 'looking the other honestly in the face', and will pay the cost of doing so.

Disempowering self: empowering others

There is more going on here, though, than the simple gesture of accepting vulnerability. Luke's witnesses to the event are extraordinary in their ordinariness. He does not involve at all the eastern sages introduced by Matthew, and all the most powerful people – the ones who would be considered to have a 'right to know' – are kept completely in the dark. Instead, the news is given only to a group of shepherds, with the clear announcement that it is *for them*. They will have the privilege of, in Irenaeus' terms, experiencing the fullness of life by 'beholding God' in the vibrant new life of a baby and its first-time parents.

For all the romantic glow bestowed on shepherds in school and church nativity plays, they were very low on the social scale. In a sense this is not news – we are accustomed to hearing of 'humble shepherds' – but in reality they were beyond humble: they were considered to be thoroughly disreputable. As far as the religious establishment of the day was concerned, shepherds had very little going for them. Unfortunately, they did have a way of leading their flocks rather indiscriminately over other people's land in search of pasture – something that endeared them to respectable citizenry about as much as do the behaviours of some nomadic groups today

– and so it was probably convenient to be able to legitimise prejudice against them on religious grounds. Their working hours made it very difficult, if not impossible, for them to participate in the cultic rituals of synagogue and temple, even if they were able to make themselves ritually pure for the occasion – and the importance of ritual purity in that culture can hardly be overstated. Their contact with blood and other unattractive by-products of animals made them ritually impure, and anyone who has observed a shepherd assisting a ewe at lambing time (Thank you for the information, James Herriot, but I really didn't need it dramatised on my TV screen at tea time!) can probably begin to imagine the level of that impurity and the distaste it generated.

That these people – straight from the fields and clearly in a state that would utterly forbid their entry into temple, synagogue or even the homes of pious Jews – were not only allowed but actively encouraged to go into the presence of God incarnate is probably one of literature's classic examples of unconditional positive regard. It is, of course, not insignificant that God incarnate was unceremoniously contained in the feeding trough in a stable at the time, surrounded by dirt, blood, faeces and who knows what other sources of ritual impurity, and as such had accepted becoming technically inadmissible to centres of worship.

A Bible passage often cited as prophesying the suffering and death of Jesus seems remarkably appropriate here:

He poured out himself to death, and was numbered with the transgressors.

Isaiah 53:12

The resonance this has traditionally found with the death of Jesus – especially when taken in context – is very easy to see. However, it seems as we read these opening chapters of Luke that Jesus was numbered with the transgressors – that he was identified with the unacceptable and unclean – from the moment of his birth and, indeed, earlier.

The Gospel according to Luke is known for its particular slant toward the dispossessed and those the world considers undeserving. It contains such texts as the magnificent Song of Mary, otherwise known as the *Magnificat*, highlighting what has been called the 'bias to the poor'.[36]

---

36 This phrase led to theologians being accused of romantically seeing all poor people through rose-tinted spectacles and making poverty a virtue. However, the great liberation theologian Gustavo Gutierrez clarified at the Lambeth Conference in 1988 that he believes God has a bias to the poor, not because the poor are good but because *God* is good.

He has shown strength with his arm;
he has scattered the proud in the thoughts of their hearts.
He has brought down the powerful from their thrones
and lifted up the lowly;
he has filled the hungry with good things,
and sent the rich away empty.

Luke 1:51-3

This theme is developed throughout the Gospel as Jesus embraces people who are ritually unclean, shares meal tables (a scandalous sign of friendship and acceptance) with social outcasts, shows respect to undervalued sections of society often represented by women and children, and generally aligns with not just the literally poor but also the dispossessed, the disapproved and the marginalised of his culture.

Luke's entire Gospel rewards careful reading with this in mind – and not only this Gospel: Matthew and Mark also contain some very revealing material. Indeed, it is those two sources that give us perhaps the most startling of all recorded conversations with Jesus. Jesus is shown in a particularly uncharacteristic and unflattering light, not only declining a request for healing but making a gratuitously harsh and derogatory remark about a woman from outside his native culture. The woman wittily twists his words and turns them back on him, upon which Jesus compliments her on her faith and grants her request for healing for her daughter (Matthew 15:21-8; Mark 7:24-30). It is surely significant that the only example in the Synoptic Gospels of someone making Jesus change his mind is one of the most unexpected – not only a despised outsider to his own religious community, but a woman into the bargain!

The light shines in the darkness

The light shines in the darkness, and the darkness did not overcome it.

John 1:5

That verse from the famous prologue of the Gospel according to John could be said to sum up much that has gone before in this chapter. It was surely not a mistake that when Christianity was brought to Britain, the pagan festival chosen to be adapted for the annual celebration of the Incarnation was the midwinter feast of Yule. Ancient traditions of midwinter festivals can be found in many cultures around the world – usually occasions that bring warmth, light and hope into the coldest, darkest and most threatening part of the year.

The fourth evangelist speaks quite modestly of this light which shines in the darkness and is not overcome – a recognition, perhaps, that the darkness remains. This is not the switching-on of a searchlight to dispel the darkness and impose the light upon the world; rather it seems much more akin to the candlelight that has become so associated with our Christmas celebrations. It's an image I love: the candle is a living flame with a warmth that is not found in the dazzle of halogen. It is a small, flickering and apparently vulnerable light that somehow, mysteriously, seems to survive and hold back the otherwise overwhelming darkness. It is a light that invites us closer, that gives hope and encouragement, but it does not simply wipe out the darkness at a stroke – rather, it enables us to live within it and even uses the darkness to enhance its own visibility.

It surely takes little imagination to see the redolence of this image for pastoral presence. There is a saying, 'It is better to light a single candle than curse the darkness.' Its origins are obscure: I have seen it attributed to ancient Chinese philosophy, to Eleanor Roosevelt, to John F. Kennedy, to the founder of Amnesty International, and I now find it is the motto of The Christophers – a society that encourages its members to use their talents for good in the world. Clearly, it is one of those sayings that so ring bells for people as to pass into common parlance. So it will be no surprise that it was frequently in my mind as I sat with people as a pastoral companion of whatever specific kind.

There is something about the candle image that is inherently vulnerable – which makes it all the more appropriate as a symbol of Incarnation when Christians celebrate immortal God's acceptance of vulnerability, and of pastoral companionship or counselling when often it can feel that the light we are trying to sustain is in danger of extinction. And that, surely, is its power. The presence of an obviously vulnerable light that yet seems to flicker defiantly in the presence of otherwise-overwhelming darkness is in some ways much more therapeutic than would be the aforementioned halogen light bursting onto the scene and dispelling the darkness at a stroke. The reality is, of course, that darkness is not something we can simply dispel from our lives; it is something with which we have to live – and the survival of the vulnerable, low-powered candle flame may symbolically encourage us to believe that that is possible for us. It is a little like the approach taken by a cognitive behavioural therapist to a client suffering from a phobia. Rather than finding ways of avoiding the darkness (or spiders, reptiles or whatever else is the bringer of anxiety), the therapist will expose the client to it in a controlled context that will enable them to build up resilience. To be transported away from the 'dark' would simply lead to a life of avoidance, increasing its power over us; to be enabled to remain in it disempowers the darkness and may even enable us to befriend it, setting us free for new and transformed life.

The image of a tiny light that overcomes darkness leads us on to another important principle of pastoral companionship.

Less is more

For God so loved the world that he didn't send a committee.

Seen on a sticker in a car window, this wry adaptation of John 3:16 is probably more profound than the signwriter realised.

If, as Christian faith claims, God chose the vulnerable, powerless form of a baby in which to become incarnate in a troubled world, then it is a ringing endorsement of the principle 'less is more'. It returns us yet again to the basic theme of this book, which is the healing power of presence even, or indeed especially, without the power to 'do something'.

'Less is more' is something that all trainee – and indeed practising – counsellors must surely have heard said many times. As I was frequently reminded by my practice supervisors, there is always more we *could* do, no matter how much has been done already – but often it is better that we do less.

Part of my counselling training involved doing 'process analyses' in which, having recorded a session with the client's permission, we would be required to type up a transcript of a section and analyse each exchange to explore what was going on for both client and counsellor. One of the most important questions we asked ourselves was whether all our interventions were necessary. Over the duration of the course it was usual for students to find that our interventions became fewer, further between, and more considered – and the counselling became more effective as the client was given more space for the internal process that counselling is meant to facilitate. We were learning the healing power of presence.

If I am honest, I found it startling to hear not only how many times I spoke during a session but how redundant most of my interventions were. That was far from an uncommon experience – it was the reason for doing the analysis – and it was often said that perhaps as many as 90 per cent of the interventions of inexperienced or trainee therapists could be omitted, to the benefit of the other. This was amply demonstrated for me in my experience with the client I mentioned earlier who used me as her 'Edgar' and, in the assessors' judgement, benefited from an almost entirely silent (even if not always by choice) presence.

Like the Hebrew Scriptures, the Christian gospel has many more treasures to offer, when viewed through this lens, than I have space to explore here. It is time to move on – to the other end of the life of Jesus on earth.

8
The dying of Jesus

Our journey has brought us to the central feature of the Christian faith – the cross. It is a symbol full of paradox and mystery, and quite incomprehensible in terms of the accepted images of all-powerful divinity swathed in glory and majesty. Just what by way of meaning can we draw from the image of crucifixion?

Here we focus upon the story (to be found in different forms toward the end of all four Gospels) of how Jesus, having provoked the religious authorities of the time beyond their capacity to tolerate, was executed by crucifixion. It was an event that his followers came to interpret not as a defeat but as a triumph, not as powerlessness but as power, and indeed as the means of their salvation.

I have chosen in the chapter title to refer to dying rather than death, because it is the manner of Jesus' dying that is of more significance here than the fact of his death. Indeed, the evangelist Mark tells us that the Roman centurion supervising the crucifixion recognised the significance:

> Now when the centurion, who stood facing him, saw that *in this way* he breathed his last, he said, 'Truly this man was God's Son!'
>
> *Mark 15:39 (my emphasis)*

Some aspects of the way the crucifixion has been interpreted are really only comprehensible from a particular faith position (which excludes even a significant number of practising and thoughtful Christians). However, like the other examples from Scripture that we have looked at, I believe the cross has wisdom and power for those who view it from a completely different perspective without having first accepted any of the traditional interpretations. I also believe, crucially, that that further wisdom is equally of value to all Christian believers.

For believers, there are a number of ways of interpreting the event and of understanding its significance for the world. What they have in common is a sense that things changed dramatically – the death of Jesus was transforming for the people there and continues to be so throughout history. Of the four classical theories of the Atonement,[37] it is fair to say that one is currently in the ascendancy – to the point

---

37 Theories exploring how the death of Jesus achieved its purpose of reconciling humanity to God – of making us once more 'at one' with our creator, hence 'atonement' ('at-one-ment').

that many people may not even be aware of the other three – and I do not propose here to enter the debate about the respective merits of those theories. I have set out in this faith section of the book to look at some of the images and stories associated with Christianity from the perspective of both the believer and the non-believer, through the shared lens of the counselling and pastoral companionship process, and that is what I propose to continue to do here.

Some of the Church's thinking about this has placed great weight on the unique nature of Jesus as the perfect, sinless Son of God. Clearly, that means we have to be careful not simply to equate the compassionate role of the pastoral companion with the suffering of Jesus, which would be grandiose by any standards. However, it is also fair to say that emphasis has had the effect of making the event effectively off limits for consideration by non-believers. If in order to find meaning in the cross of Jesus one must approach it from a position of theism, then the danger is that important wisdom will be lost to the world – including to Christians as we focus solely upon the faith-based interpretations. It also becomes very difficult to talk about it at all without arousing the suspicion that one is trying to convert someone.

I have no intention of indulging in such grandiosity as to equate the work that I and other pastoral companions have done with the unique, once-for-all act of redemption! However, if we leave that aspect aside and look at the cross through the rather different lens of pastoral companionship or counselling, we find other insights. These insights, far from detracting from the faith of Christians, actually add further layers of significance and enhancement.

A cautionary note is required here, though. It would be dangerously easy to make a simple identification between the figure of Jesus and that of the pastoral companion, so that the latter takes on a kind of 'mythic hero' role, which is more inappropriate than I have words to describe! As we have already seen when considering the birth narratives, incarnational faith calls and enables us to see the presence of the divine in *all humanity* – in the other as much as in the companion, and the case of Marion is an example of the other offering a revelation of the divine to the companion. From a biblical perspective, it may also be helpful to remember that in a famous passage in Matthew, Jesus specifically identified himself not with the pastoral companion but the other (Matthew 25:31-46).

Also inappropriate is any idea that as pastoral companions we are called to gratuitous suffering. There is nothing glamorous or heroic about suffering *per se* – the concept of a suffering God who chooses to inhabit the pain of the world, far from valorising, raises a howl of protest.

Having, hopefully, clarified those points, my intention is to look at the crucifixion narratives as motifs of God's way of being present to creation, and to ask what it can say to us about our presence with one another and how that can have healing power.

I propose to think in terms of three headings: the concept of the wounded healer; foolish wisdom; and the temptations of power and powerlessness. As we do that, it is well to be clear about some of the dangers in thinking about the cross in connection with pastoral companionship.

To reinforce the point already made, the cross is emphatically not about gratuitous suffering. Christians are called to be ready to 'take up the cross', but that does not mean we go looking for one to hang on. The Gospel writers show Jesus only accepting the cross when the time and the purpose were right, and specifically avoiding danger at other times in his ministry. The giving of his life had to be meaningful, and there was no way he was going to become a martyr just for the sake of it. There is nothing intrinsically virtuous about suffering.

Anyone who has listened seriously to the stories of distressed people will also know that it is emphatically not simplistically the case that 'What doesn't kill you makes you stronger'. Certainly, some of us may experience increased resilience as we come through testing experiences, but that is not universal by any means. I speak with some passion born out of not inconsiderable contact with people seriously damaged by suffering, probably beyond full recovery, and too many who sought the only release they could by ending their lives. After all that, I hope I may be forgiven if I display a certain intolerance towards simplistic platitudes about suffering being good for people!

Finally, it is probably worth reminding ourselves that we are talking about pastoral companionship – not counselling (although we have found insights from that discipline helpful) – and it is important to recognise the limitations in our role. As well as a different level of training, skills and experience, the pastoral companion will usually have less in the way of support systems available than specialists working in the professional field, and should be ready to recognise when the pain of the other is beyond the companion's capacity to share. At this point there must be support on hand through supervision and the facility, if appropriate, for onward referral to a specialist service. We have a duty to our families and to ourselves not to get in over our heads.

Let's look at some helpful insights that the cross offers in connection with pastoral companionship.

The wounded healer

This concept of the wounded healer has become widely known, and many people intuitively assume it relates to Jesus and the Christian claim that his suffering had healing power for the world.

> But he was wounded for our transgressions,
> crushed for our iniquities;
> upon him was the punishment that made us whole,
> and by his bruises we are healed.
>
> *Isaiah 53:5*

Clearly the term 'wounded healer' is very apt in that context, but it has also been coined by at least two others in more recent times. The psychologist Carl Jung[38] famously used it to express his conviction that it is our own woundedness that impels us to seek to heal others. It later became more widely known as the title of a book by Henri M. Nouwen, the central point of which is not that our wounds can be healing for others *per se*, but rather that we who seek to be a healing presence to others must begin from an acknowledgement of our own woundedness.

There is no doubt in my mind that, as Jung says, our own experience of being wounded plays a large part in motivating us to want to help in the healing of others, but it is, of course, one source of motivation among many. Personal congruence should make us all aware of other, more complex and sometimes ulterior motives.

What neither Jung nor Nouwen says is that our woundedness is a qualification for fixing others. A popular idea, supposing we have found some deep wisdom within our suffering, is that if we simply impart that wisdom to others, it will heal them, too. That is an idea that deserves to be given a very wide berth. It would be a most unusual – unique, I should say – person who reached a mature age without some significant experience of being wounded, but that does not in itself make us all healers – still less founts of eternal wisdom.

A slightly different (and more modest) interpretation is that our woundedness in itself can have healing value for others, and while there is some important truth in that idea, it should not be treated simplistically. The reality is much more complex, and simply exposing others to our wounds *per se* is at best not guaranteed to have positive effects and at worst very dangerous for the well-being of both parties. Doing that may sometimes (very rarely) be appropriate,

---

38 Jung, Carl, 'The Psychology of the Transference', *The Practice of Psychotherapy* (Ark Paperbacks).

but it demands a high degree of not only empathy but also personal congruence to know when those times are and when (which is most of the time) we should keep our troubles firmly to ourselves. We shall consider this further in a moment.

Nouwen's point is rather more subtle. He says that if we are to be a resource for others' healing then we must begin by being *aware* of our own wounds and come alongside people as companions in their distress rather than stand over them as examples of wholeness.

In my work with Eleanor, it became clear that a very significant cause of her distress lay in trying to live up to a shining example of stoicism and invulnerability that was as destructive as it was unrealistic. What finally enabled her to face and live through her grief was the companionship of someone who was also wounded – and vulnerable – and knew it.

We should also be clear that this is not about the fallacy that we can only help others if we have exactly the same wounds. The precise nature and extent of the wounds inevitably will be different, but the essential point is the effect that the companion's *awareness of their own woundedness* has on the relationship.

It might be seen from all this that the wounded healer concept has much to do with the two core conditions we have seen defined as empathy and congruence. Our ability to empathise with another is closely linked to our awareness of our own woundedness, while personal congruence should make us aware of how it affects our part in the process. It is to be hoped that these personal qualities will enable us to avoid the trap of what Nouwen calls 'spiritual exhibitionism' – putting our own troubles on display under the pretext of helping others.

Spiritual exhibitionism

We should look at this carefully because this is, in fact, just how the crucifixion of Jesus has been, and too often still is, used. In the specific context of religious faith, the image of the cross has huge value. To put it simply, I might almost say that it is the only image that really helps me believe in God at all, but when it is taken as an example of how we should present ourselves to the world, it becomes something very different. Let's look at it briefly from both of these angles.

The Christian faith position is that, in the man Jesus, God entered into the depths of human suffering. This is presented both as a one-off act of atonement-sacrifice – a powerful idea that is outside the scope of this book to explore in depth – and as a representation of the way God is (a profoundly compelling idea that is central to pastoral theology and to this discussion). To put it very simply, many people find a God who willingly enters into the pain of the world at its deepest level profoundly more helpful than the invulnerable God of Platonism, who stays remote from creation and directs things from a safe distance. (This sadly infected Christian thinking at a formative stage, but that is for another book.)

In this way, it is not hard to see how the image of the cross would transform our view of God and cause us to reconsider all our preconceived ideas. Many people, including this writer, have found that in doing so they encounter a God to whom they can relate and who can help them. However, that is a long way from what Nouwen describes as 'spiritual exhibitionism', which arises from the belief either that our suffering is some kind of badge of honour to be displayed for others to admire or – and this is where it becomes of particular concern to us – that being exposed to it will be a quick fix for the pain of another. Acknowledging our own woundedness is one thing; parading it gratuitously is something else entirely. Very far from helping, it can in all kinds of ways be profoundly damaging to the other. Here is just a representative sample of those ways:

- The other might come to feel protective towards us and thus feel unable to mention things that are of crucial importance to them out of fear that we might find them hurtful.
- The other might discern that we are in reality more preoccupied with our own pain than with theirs, and feel undermined.
- It might be construed as wanting in some way to take ownership of the client's experience (what I have heard graphically described as 'taking a package holiday in someone else's grief').
- To equate our feelings with those of the other is a failure to honour the uniqueness of their experience.
- The other has come to us to share their feelings – not to be obliged to contemplate ours.
- It might turn the session into a competition: 'My wound's more gruesome than yours.'
- It might – and here we enter into another area (that of self-care) – so affect the companion's well-being as to make them less able to be available to the other. Maintaining our own well-being in order to be fit to practise safely is a specific ethical requirement of counsellors and pastoral companions.

The list could go on and on, but hopefully the message is clear: our focus is on the other, and any temptation to assume centre stage is by definition an attempt to displace the other from where they should rightfully be. This, of course, is unethical as well as counterproductive, and not at all in keeping with the 'hospitality' that Nouwen believes to be at the heart of the healing process.[39] It is in the act of hospitality – of giving space to another – that we facilitate their healing (not for nothing does 'hospitality' share its root with 'hospital' and 'hospice'). Our role is always to give space to the other – and to make that a healing space for them. Elbowing our way into it with our own ailments on display – however mistakenly well-intentioned that may be – is not part of the process.

The primary benefit of the concept of the wounded healer, then, is of value in pastoral companionship in terms of how it *affects the demeanour of the companion* as they come alongside a fellow human being who is also wounded, in a state of personal congruence and able to engage empathically with them.

Foolish wisdom

God's foolishness is wiser than human wisdom and God's weakness is stronger than human strength.

Consider your own call, brothers and sisters: not many of you were wise by human standards, not many were powerful, not many were of noble birth. But God chose what is foolish in the world to shame the wise; God chose what is weak in the world to shame the strong.

1 Corinthians 1:25-7

It is easy – and therefore sadly not unknown – for this passage to be used in Christian circles to make simplistic (as distinct from simple) foolishness a virtue. So the first thing I need to say here is that 'being a fool for Christ' is not a matter of believing six impossible things before breakfast!

What is being described here is not gullibility, but rather the discernment of a radically different wisdom so contrary to accepted conventions as to be regarded as foolish. It is the wisdom of the wise fool.

Historically, that concept has embraced such figures as the court jester and the character of the fool in some Shakespeare plays, tolerated by the powerful for their entertainment value and, as in the case of Shakespeare's King Lear, for example, empowered by that very toleration to say the unsayable that others dare not utter for fear of the consequences. As another Shakespearean fool put it, 'Better a witty fool than a foolish wit' – a line I heard rendered in

---

39 Nouwen, Henri J. M., *The Wounded Healer* (Darton, Longman & Todd 1994), p.89.

one production as 'Better a wise fool than a foolish sage'.[40] To use a different analogy – from Hans Christian Andersen – when everyone has swallowed (because it is the 'wise' thing to do) the story about the Emperor's New Clothes, there is a great need for the small boy who hasn't heard what he's supposed to believe, to give those people the freedom to admit to their awareness that the potentate is starkers!

A direct benefit of the wise fool's position is the ability to highlight the weakness of conventional wisdom with something radically different. This might be because of the fool's unique position in being able to move in circles of power without being corrupted by it, having none of his own and no prospects – which, of course, paradoxically gives him a very particular kind of power. He is the outsider on the inside, and his view is different from those of the people caught up in the power play. Sometimes, as Lennon and McCartney observed, the fool sees the reality behind the immediately apparent – the 'blindingly obvious' at which the perceptions of conventional wisdom stop.

> The fool on the hill
> sees the sun going down,
> and the eyes in his head
> see the world spinning round.[41]

In terms of the Christian revelation of God, we have already seen how the apparently foolish notion of a God who suffers pain and renounces power even to the point of humiliation (a concept still deeply offensive to many religious believers) can be seen to offer a radical wisdom. As Dietrich Bonhoeffer, the German pastor martyred in the concentration camps, observed, 'Only the suffering God can help'.[42]

In recent years, the unmissable opportunity for me to explore this theme in worship arose when Good Friday fell on 1 April – All Fools' Day. The theme of the service simply had to be 'The fool on the hill' and the playing of John Lennon's recording of that title played a central part.

Jesus, the 'fool on the hill', sees beyond the simply obvious – as in the setting sun – to the deeper reality that it manifests – the spinning of the earth. More literally, he sees beyond the apparently obvious failure and humiliation to envision the possibility of redemption, and to open our eyes to it also.

Much of this book has, indeed, been about 'foolish wisdom'. In the 1950s, when his ideas were being explored by psychologists and psychotherapists, Carl Rogers had a hard time convincing his peers

---

40 Shakespeare, William, *Twelfth Night*, Act 1 Scene 5.
41 Paul McCartney, John Lennon, 'The fool on the hill', copyright © Sony/ATV Tunes LLC.
42 Bonhoeffer, Dietrich, *Letters and Papers from Prison* (SCM Press 2001).

that a 'non-directive' approach, as it was then considered, was viable. The very notion that 'it is the client who knows'[43] seemed foolish to the point of incomprehensible. Why on earth would a person who knows the direction they should take come for therapy at all? Rogers was seeing beyond the setting sun to the spinning of the earth, recognising the blocks that were preventing that knowledge being recognised and used by the client and discovering new ways in which they might be removed.

In terms of Christian spirituality, the connections are to be found almost everywhere. The concept of a humble and vulnerable – let alone suffering and dying – God that lies at its heart, and expressed with particular power in the birth and death narratives of Jesus, is – on the face of it – foolish. However, when we stand alongside the fool on the hill and see things through those very different eyes, we see beyond the apparently obvious to the deeper wisdom, the greater reality behind.

If there is anyone who should be able to take the wisdom of the fool seriously, it surely should be a Christian – one whose very faith is founded on the foolish wisdom of God, and whose faith symbol is the emblem of it!

Many of the people who come to us in distress have already heard far too much 'wisdom' from others. Someone who will simply be there, congruently, empathically and unconditionally, can create a therapeutic space in the midst of all that and enable undiscerned realities masked by the assumptions of conventional wisdom to emerge.

The temptations of power and of powerlessness

> Those who passed by derided him, shaking their heads and saying, 'If you are the Son of God, come down from the cross.' In the same way the chief priests also, along with the scribes and elders, were mocking him, saying, 'He saved others; he cannot save himself. He is the King of Israel; let him come down from the cross now, and we will believe in him. He trusts in God; let God deliver him now, if he wants to; for he said, "I am God's Son."' The bandits who were crucified with him also taunted him in the same way.
>
> *Matthew 27:39-44*

In this passage, the Gospel writer Matthew graphically portrays the humiliation heaped upon (and doubtless felt by) the powerless Jesus

---

43 Rogers, *On Becoming a Person*, p.11.

in his dying hours. It is not difficult to imagine something of the despair and loneliness of the experience. I propose now to look a little deeper – to put on the spectacles of the fool on the hill and to see behind the obvious to find deeper wisdom. Before that, though, there is another aspect of the humiliation that I want to bring out, and then we shall examine the scene from the viewpoint of a counsellor or pastoral companion.

It is important that, as we read these words, whatever our personal faith position, we try to do so through the eyes of the narrator, Matthew. Matthew's assumption almost undoubtedly would have been what we now know as traditional Christian orthodoxy – that Jesus, as God incarnate, had the power to remove himself from the cross and that all that kept him there was commitment to his mission, the redemption of the world. For the incarnate Son of God who earlier in his earthly career had walked on water, controlled the weather with a word of command, healed the incurably sick, miraculously fed hungry masses and even raised the dead back to life, surely dealing with a few nails would be a walk in the park! Jesus, Matthew tells us, *chose* to remain on the cross through all this. (Again, we do not need here to go into the theology and philosophy behind that idea. The question we need to ask is, given that he wrote from that faith position, what was Matthew particularly saying when he decided to include this incident in his narrative?) Looking at it through his eyes brings us to a subject of enormous relevance to counsellors and pastoral companions: the temptations of power and of powerlessness.

In reading this section of Matthew's Gospel, we realise we have actually been in this territory before. Let's flip back through the pages to the beginning of Jesus' ministry and the well-known episode of the temptation of Jesus in the wilderness in Matthew 4:1-11.

The three temptations were:

- Turn stones into bread to satisfy hunger.
- Jump from a pinnacle of the temple to attract attention.
- Worship me (Satan) and I'll give you the world.

Strange though it may seem, these are highly relevant to the subject we are considering. Let's take a look at each in turn.

1. Turn stones into bread

There are two temptations here. Jesus has gone into the desert, Matthew specifically tells us, to fast as well as to pray. In that tradition, the three went together:

- The desert as a place of meditation where, free from distractions and with life stripped to its bare essentials, he could listen to God his Father.
- The discipline of not indulging the appetites was intended to help focus the mind on spiritual matters.
- Active prayer, made the more concentrated and effective by those factors.

Jesus, though, being possessed of divine powers, has his very own 'Get out of gaol free' card: he could simply turn the stones to bread and satisfy his appetite. So the temptations are twofold, at least: misuse power for his own ends and exploit the benefits of a privilege not available to the lesser mortals whose life he claims to share (well, no one would ever know, so he could easily maintain the pretence); and to place his own desire for food above the concentrated discipline of focusing on God – who in this context is 'other'. Both these temptations, he resists.

2. Jump off the temple

This is a good one – and very familiar to clergy in particular who are familiar with the problem: How do I get people to listen to what I have to say? There seems to be a simple solution (quick fix): do something spectacular; pull a stunt that will grab attention.

There's just one snag: it doesn't work! In fact, it's counterproductive.

I remember years ago hearing a number of worshippers in a church enthuse about the preacher who had recently conducted their worship. He was most unusual – and very entertaining. He had begun his sermon by turning a cartwheel, simply in order to gain the congregation's attention.

I asked all the people who described this incident to me what the preacher had gone on to say. Not one of them could remember. The memory of the stunt had stuck, but it had distracted them completely from the message. Some people may still remember the famous Cinzano Bianco adverts which starred the late great Leonard Rossiter pouring a glass of the beverage down the front of Joan Collins' dress. It was a highly entertaining advert, and people would refrain from using the commercial break for tea-making if they thought it might be on. Just one problem – many people remembered the advert but forgot the name of the product! Matthew shows us Satan craftily attempting to sabotage Jesus' mission by making a tempting and distracting suggestion.

3. 'Worship me!'

I don't think for one moment that there was ever any thought that Jesus would become a card-carrying satanist. The temptation was more subtle than that. Jesus has been transported in his vision to a high mountain from where he can see all the glorious kingdoms of the world, and he is told that he can have it all. His mission is to establish the kingdom of God on earth, and this would give him a head start. 'Worshipping the devil' in this case would in practical terms be about expediency: forget the stuff about a radical alternative – offer people what they want. Adopt the old ways, conform yourself to the world, do whatever it takes to get power, and then once you've got it, you can do all the things you *really* want to do. Why go the long way when you can take a short cut?

It does not take a cynic to see the political connections.

If you want to bring peace, then raise a mighty army and frighten everybody into peaceful behaviour. Humanity has been trying to do that since recorded history began, and probably before.

Why bother to try to convince people of your values and principles? Just promise them the world, pretend to be whoever and whatever they want, and then when you've got the power you can bring out the real agenda.

Matthew makes it clear that Jesus kept his integrity through all of these temptations. He stayed true to himself and to his purpose. And that probably seemed fine and dandy in the heady idealism and high hopes of his approach to ministry. Now, Matthew shows us Jesus hanging humiliated – and in agony beyond description – on the cross, and in effect reliving those temptations in the five beguilingly simple words, 'Come down from the cross'. In other words:

- 'Turn stones into bread': forget the mission – put your own needs first and use your divine powers for your own benefit.

- 'Jump off the temple tower': do something spectacular – that'll show them. Why put up with all this when you could just prove yourself and have them eating out of your hand?

- 'Worship the devil': forget the divine plan – it's obviously in tatters. Use a bit of good old-fashioned worldly power and bring this lot to heel. They'll follow you anywhere if you do that.

For the divine Son of God who, having renounced his power, was presumably quite free to take it back again, those temptations would be almost overwhelming. That is not difficult to imagine. But what does all this mean to a pastoral companion or counsellor?

Being there

We could say that from the perspective of Christian belief, the crucifixion is God's way of 'being there'. Having renounced the use of power in order to facilitate relationship, as we saw earlier, there is now nothing to do but to 'trust the process' – to trust that, even in this extreme situation, 'just being there' will be enough.

One does not need to have worked with people experiencing the most extreme forms of distress and disturbance to know the feeling of sheer powerlessness that is all too often the lot of the counsellor or pastoral companion. Sometimes in my own ministry the sense of despair has hung heavily in the very air in the room – a despair that I was powerless to change but felt called in whatever way I could to inhabit as a healing and hopeful presence. The temptations are very real:

- This is not literally my world – I've entered it for the sake of the other – I don't have to stay in it – I can make it easier for myself and maybe the other does not need to know.
- Perhaps I can use the difficult silences to think about something else (mentally design a piece of furniture[44] or ponder my next book, for example) rather than focus on the other.
- Do I really have to sit here looking and feeling so incompetent? Maybe there's something I can say just to get myself off the hook? It doesn't need to be of real value – just some nice, easy, wise-sounding platitude that will stop me feeling so humiliated. Why should I stay with the process when it doesn't seem to be working?
- These feel like extreme circumstances to me – maybe I would be justified in abandoning the process I'm committed to and finding some kind of short cut – something that will make the other feel better (if only in the short term). I can deal with any issues that arise later, but right now I just need to get myself of the hook.

Of course, I don't really believe any of that – but in the extreme of apparent hopelessness and powerlessness it would be easy to convince myself that I do. It is to be hoped that for most pastoral companions the extreme cases will rarely or never be experienced. For those in some specialist fields, they simply go with the territory. However, while there will be differences of degree, anyone entering into the distress of another will experience at some level the temptation to 'come down from the cross', along

---

44 Cabinetmaking is my passion and chief leisure activity, and this particular temptation was very strong!

with the sense of failure, powerlessness and humiliation that makes it all but irresistible.

The form that it takes will vary. It may be literally to end the session and physically get out of that place (one that I have felt too many times to remember, and while I never actually did it, there were undoubtedly times when I checked my watch more often than was appropriate). More probable is the temptation to prove that I am special – that I do have wisdom to offer – by some kind of totally inappropriate intervention that arises out of the depth of my preoccupation not with the other but with myself. I suspect I am not the only pastoral companion or counsellor to have given in to that one at some point.

That, for me, was when the spiritual power of the cross was most vital.

Again, we do not need to consider the various ways in which theologians have sought to explain the 'how' of it, but it is the case that for those who most closely witnessed the gruesome spectacle – and the personal grief and trauma – of the cross, and for countless thousands who have contemplated it in history, the conviction has been that precisely because Jesus did not come down from the cross, something transformational happened that could not have been achieved in any other way.

It is not over-dramatising to say that I have clung to the image of the cross and the silence of the crucified Jesus many times in the vestry or therapy room. This is a powerful image for Christian pastoral companions, and my experience has been that if we can stay there – and usually stay silent at that time, and keep the focus on the other – something transformational can happen. However, we do need to trust the process. It almost certainly won't happen in that session, and it might not happen until we have lived through the scenario many times, with the disappointment and humiliation (and with them the temptations) building as time goes on.

I'm reminded again of the conversation a fellow student on my counselling course had with the tutor:

> 'But what do you do when absolutely nothing is happening?'
> 'It is impossible for two people to be in a room together and nothing be happening.'

We should never underestimate the internal processes that continue in the silences. We should never underestimate the power of 'just being there'. And we should never underestimate the healing power of presence.

The choice would be a fine thing

There is more in this, however. Our focus has been on the image of the crucified Jesus and what that may hold for us – but there are other crosses in this story, and the occupants of those are subject to none of Jesus' temptations, simply because they have no choice in the matter.

All four Gospels refer to the criminals crucified with Jesus. Luke and John specifically state that they are on either side, with Jesus at the centre of the tableau of suffering. What distinguishes Jesus from these other figures? Some will answer very quickly that Jesus is innocent while the other two are not. Luke certainly seems to add veracity to this, through the mouth of the one whom tradition has called the 'penitent thief', but the other three evangelists give these characters no dialogue at all.

For me, the distinction is emphatically not between guilt and innocence. That would be a very dangerous line of thought to pursue in this discussion, as there is enough stigma applied to suffering people without our sanctifying it here! For me, the distinction is as I have already intimated: the difference between having and not having choice. Whatever the modern reader may make of it, the Gospel writers undoubtedly believed that Jesus accepted the cross as a matter of choice. That belief is central to traditional Christian theology. So what does it mean to us to see his crucifixion set in the context (two Gospels actually make it the centre) of suffering that is not accepted but imposed – where the suffering people have no choice?

Let us consider the image: one person who chooses to be in the place of pain, portrayed at the centre of choiceless suffering. Such a presence highlights not only the pain but also the injustice of the scene. Could it be that the people crucified alongside Jesus represent the suffering of a world that has no choice to accept it – and at the heart of the scene is the God who chooses to be part of that and to remain there, come what may?

I am reminded of the years of Nelson Mandela's imprisonment on Robben Island, and particularly the last months in which he repeatedly refused to accept release. The Apartheid government had realised that his release was vital to their own survival – the prospect of what might happen if he died in prison was beyond contemplation. The world was treated to the spectacle of the prisoner utterly turning the tables on his ostensibly powerful captors by forcing them to negotiate his release on his terms. Mandela was not simply going to let them off the hook by walking out and defusing the much bigger issue – which was the suffering not of himself but of the people he represented. He would stay in that prison until such time as his leaving would mean not only his own liberation but that of his people, too.

For the traditional Christian believer, here is powerful imagery that resonates with the traditional interpretations of the death of Jesus. For the non-theist, or indeed for those Christians who interpret that event differently, the image is nonetheless powerful. The one who chooses to stay among those who have no choice becomes a symbol not only of divine love but also of hope and of protest. Their presence gives resonance to the silent screams of the choiceless and voiceless.

It is well to remind ourselves of an important point here. The figure of the crucified Jesus is being used as an image of a way of being present to others. The danger is that it is a hair's breadth away from seeing the pastoral companion as a 'divine' figure. Let us remember what has been observed before: all humanity is in the image of God – not just powerful, choice-endowed humanity – and as noted earlier, Jesus himself is said to have identified himself not with the visitor/companion but with the other who is also created in the image of God. My use of this image in this way does, then, have certain dangers, of which we need to be very aware.

To return to the matter under consideration, there are countless people who have no choice but to accept the terrible hand that life has dealt them. It is not about guilt, or about wisdom; it is about choice or the lack of it. The feelings engendered are wide ranging but will often include a sense of worthlessness that is compounded by their experience of isolation. For those people, the simple fact of someone's willingness to 'be there' can be life changing – but only if it can be sustained. Parents who have fostered or adopted children with long histories of rejection know about this. The child will be convinced that rejection is just around the corner. No one else has stuck with them, and this new do-gooder will be no different. Well, if it's going to happen, better get it over with! The foster parents' commitment will be tested to destruction by behaviour specifically intended to do exactly that.

It is not hard to imagine the feelings of people who feel trapped by circumstances, who would undoubtedly 'come down from the cross' in an instant, and who find themselves joined in that place by someone who has the very power they crave but chooses not to use it! It is surely no surprise that in their Gospel accounts, Matthew, Mark and Luke all have the people crucified with him turn on Jesus. Luke even puts the words of derision into the mouth of one of them: 'Aren't you someone special? Well save yourself, then – and us while you're at it!' (Luke 23:39, my paraphrase).

I have worked with people who have taken a long time to accept that I'm serious about being there. (I even continued my work with one client as a volunteer long after my retirement because I was determined not to confirm the negative expectation!) I have worked with people who, after years of let-downs and desertions, simply needed a 'rock' – someone who would be there come what may and, no matter how much scorn was poured on him, would choose to stay.

Sadly, the financial and other constraints on the NHS make that kind of commitment prohibitively expensive – especially where seriously long-term mental health issues are concerned – and so the cynical expectations are, sadly, too often confirmed. It is no easy thing to commit to this for the sake of another. For churches to offer it, through a system of pastoral companionship, would require serious improvements in the training and supervision currently available. But in what better way might the Church show itself to be serious about the commitment it regularly expresses in words to 'take up the cross'?

What was that phrase again? Oh, yes: the healing power of presence.

9
Resurrection

Precisely what happened in the time following the crucifixion and the extent to which we can even know that in any case are matters of heated debate within Christian communities, let alone beyond. However, most of us can agree that *something did* happen.

Whether the event was physical, spiritual or psychological is and will doubtless remain a hot topic, but somehow, within a remarkably short time after the crucifixion, the intended deterrent effect of that gruesome execution was subverted into the last thing that the authorities wanted – indeed, exactly what they had been trying to avoid. The followers of Jesus, far from hiding themselves away (although they had apparently done that for a short time), were out on the streets proclaiming in the face of the very authorities who had engineered the crucifixion that Jesus was alive and, more than that, exalted to the position of Godhead. This was worse than reversal – this was revolution!

Without entering the doctrinal debate, I want to take a little time to consider the significance of the resurrection narratives for the counsellor or pastoral companion, first in quite general terms and then by examining three specific stories from the appearances of the risen Jesus.

Death to complacency!

The narrative of resurrection – and the clear indications of its effect on the followers of Jesus – stands first and foremost as a great, resonant, defiant 'No' to the negative forces of oppression, whatever form they take – whether in the arenas of religion, politics, education or health and well-being. History tells us – and in this instance it is clearly a historic reality – that those forces did not have the final word over the Jesus movement. A gruesome, hideous and shameful public execution, the parading of the obvious human frailty of the pretender and the clear message that such would be the likely fate of any who followed: all of that had been used not only to silence Jesus himself but (in keeping with Roman policy on internal law and order) also to ensure that his movement and his ideas would die with him. The formidable powers of the Roman empire (spurred on by the religious authorities) had done their utmost. And they had failed. Whatever position one takes with regard to the nature of the resurrection, we cannot deny that the movement continued and flourished, as its presence is a clear reality around the world.

What this amounts to, then, is a ringing declaration that the powers of negativity and oppression do not have the last word. In places where people are oppressed – by whatever phenomena – resurrection faith writes in huge letters across the scene, 'This is not the last word: it does not need to be this way.' We have seen the power of that in history all down the ages. I have already mentioned experiences in South Africa, in Latin America and in troubled Belfast – and daily we may witness on the news people of faith (not necessarily Christian or even religious) raising that banner in places of fear and injustice. For a Christian observer, this is the power of resurrection.

I have mentioned a number of clients with whom I have worked who had seemed to be in a hopeless state. Although my clinical colleagues were too respectful to use the words, it was pretty clear at times that they considered me (with very good reason, from their perspective) to be naive or even fanciful in terms of my hopes for some of the clients. I remember a particular nurse – one for whom I had and retain the highest respect both for her clinical skills and her human qualities – who would try sometimes to warn me against over-optimism and disappointment. 'You must be realistic, Michael. I've known this patient for many years longer than you. She *will* kill herself one day – not may, but will. It's only a matter of time.'

This was a nurse who was rightly loved and respected by many of the patients as well as her colleagues, and I imply no criticism of her in this anecdote – indeed, it was in no small measure to her credit that the patient concerned was still alive at all. She would not give up on the patient as long as there was breath, and she certainly was not asking me to, but she was simply trying to keep my feet on the ground. That is an interesting metaphor: I once heard ministry described as having one's head in the clouds and one's feet on the ground. Perhaps that was my role – and the nurse was taking care of the grounded end!

I valued enormously this nurse's experience and expertise – as well as her compassionate desire to keep me grounded – but my head was, in the best possible sense, in the clouds. Although I saw some clients in the capacity of counsellor, I was first and foremost a chaplain – that was my job title, and my personal and professional priority. Before and above all else I was there to witness to *resurrection faith* – that was my calling. Resurrection faith did not give me certainty that I was right and the nurse wrong, but it did give me a living hope – a hope grounded in the conviction that the patient's illness, her history, her current situation, and all else that was oppressive to her, did not need to have the final say.

'This is not the last word: it does not need to be this way.'

This is not to suggest that I possessed (or even had access to) some special power. Like any other professional in this field, I felt the disappointment and the pain of failure all too many times. The journey to new life makes huge demands not only upon the pastoral companion, minister or therapist but also upon the other, and there were some who, for various reasons, did not feel able to continue the journey. The nurse (among others) was right to keep me grounded – but happy as it turned out not be proved correct in her prediction. The patient concerned is one we encountered earlier, whom I have called Eleanor.

At about this time, my wife was employed in a different but related field, as a college lecturer working with students with Profound and Multiple Learning Disabilities (PMLD). The unit where she taught was in the same grounds as one of the hospitals I covered, and insofar as their healthcare was concerned, her students came within my responsibility as chaplain, which gave me the great privilege of observing the work done there. It was almost uncanny to hear the similar conversations taking place. The carers who often accompanied the students to the unit had been caring for them for a long time, and would sometimes say of a student in relation to a particular activity, 'Oh, he can't do that – you'll never get him to manage it – is there something easier for him to do?' Those remonstrations became less frequent as the care workers became accustomed to seeing those barriers overcome. My wife's way of being as a lecturer, like mine as chaplain, was characterised by resurrection faith – in her case reinforced by a lifetime of overcoming her own very different obstacles – and that faith stood as protest and as hope on behalf of her students.

'This is not the last word: it does not need to be this way.'

Now both retired, we will sometimes be out in the town or maybe visiting a local beauty spot and hear the delighted cry, 'Jean! It's Jean!' as one of her past students, on an outing with some bemused carers, recognises her. Learning difficulties they may have – but many of them have never forgotten the lecturer who believed against all the weight of evidence that things could be different for them.

There are, of course, many examples in the public awareness – people who have suffered brain damage and been thought beyond recovery but whose families have dedicated months of their time to reading to them, playing music to them, talking about old times or simply holding their hand. Like everything else in this book, it's not a quick fix or a guarantee, but there are enough of those people who have experienced some degree of recovery to give credibility to the cry of protest:

'This is not the last word: it does not need to be this way.'

Biblical resurrection narratives

According to the Gospel narratives, some of the disciples went on the Sunday morning to the tomb where Jesus had been buried, to complete the hurried burial rituals, having observed the Sabbath rest on the Saturday as the law required. There, the Gospels tell us, they found the tomb empty and all had some kind of experience whereby they learned of his resurrection. The exact nature of the experience differs from Gospel to Gospel, but they do have some things in common that are of interest.

In all the Gospels there is a strong sense that things have changed profoundly. This resurrection is not a simple 'happy ever after' in which things may continue as they have always been. In that sense, however one reads the Gospel narratives, it is important to say that Jesus did not 'come back from the dead' but went through death and out the other side. The former is resuscitation, the latter resurrection. The former is exemplified by Lazarus (John 11:1-44), who presumably later died, and the latter by Jesus. The combined witness of the Gospels is that living in resurrection faith is not about a return to life as it was, but neither is it about simply escaping this world into a better one. It is about new and transformed life *within* the world as it is. However we cut it, life is never going to be exactly the same again. In some ways it may well be more challenging, even threatening – but it will be illumined by the resurrection experience.

Jesus meets Mary Magdalene (John 20:11-18)

In the Gospel according to John, Mary Magdalene meets Jesus but does not immediately recognise him and assumes him to be the gardener. It is in his speaking of her name that he becomes identifiable.

There are various theories about who exactly Mary Magdalene was – and none of them is completely convincing. For centuries she has been portrayed in a less-than-rosy light by Christian tradition, which might arise from the reference in Luke 8:2 to Jesus having exorcised seven demons from her. Against that background, it is interesting that the evangelist shows the speaking of her name to be the event that prompts recognition. What is significant about her being called by her name? Might it be that the respectful use of her name marks out Jesus from the generality of men in their dealings with her? It's impossible to know, but at the least it does no harm to speculate that this might be an example of Jesus 'looking the other honestly in the face' in the respectful way he deals with those whom respectable society treats very differently. Whether or not this resonates with John's subtext, it certainly does with many of the encounters between Jesus and marginalised people mentioned in the Gospels in general. However, there is a more substantive point to be raised about this narrative.

At the moment of recognition, John shows us Jesus doing something strange: Mary reaches out to him, but he stops her: 'Do not hold on to me' – or probably more accurately, 'Do not cling to me'. Jesus goes on to say that he is moving on – returning 'to my God and your God'. There is something here, is there not, about not clinging to old ways, old dependencies? John's Christology is very much focused on the exaltation of Jesus, and the message to his readers is about that. However, we may also detect in this episode a challenge to Mary and through her to the disciples: don't try and cling to the way things are – this event changes everything.

It is not inappropriate to speak of the work of pastoral companions in terms of new and different life beyond the process. We have seen examples of people for whom that was a reality – but it was a challenging one for them and for those who shared their lives. The end of therapy meant letting go and moving on, but not into a wonderful Utopian existence. They would be living in the same world but in the light of their experience; living in the world that is still shadowed by pain, by injustice, by exploitation, but with the radically life-transforming knowledge that, *'This is not the last word: it does not need to be this way.'* They would be living (although not necessarily as card-carrying Christians) by 'resurrection faith' in a world (and perhaps a home and family) that remained as dysfunctional as it had ever been. It is not hard to imagine that that would be not only exhilarating but also challenging and, while full of possibility, could also lead to conflict – as, of course, the followers of Jesus experienced.

Go back to Galilee (Mark 16:1-8)

The evangelist known as Mark expresses this differently. Without entering into the debate, I am for our purposes accepting the view widely held among scholars that the original Gospel ended at Mark 16:8 with the angel's announcement of the resurrection to the disciples and the injunction to go back to Galilee where they would find Jesus. With this device, Mark is directing his readers back to the beginning of his Gospel to read again but in a new light – the light of resurrection faith.

To the disciples at the time, the challenge would have been greater: go back to the place where all the negatives still hold sway and live there *in the light of resurrection*. They would be living out their new faith among people who did not share their experience, in a place where the same oppressive forces were still at work. There they were to live, and to proclaim in the face of all that, *'This is not the last word: it does not need to be this way.'* This would be a life characterised by hope – a defiant hope that looks the oppressive, life-denying forces in the face and refuses to accept that they have ultimate power.

The Emmaus Road (Luke 24:13-35)

There is another aspect of this 'going back' that is uniquely illustrated by Luke. On the Sunday evening following Good Friday's crucifixion, two disciples who have somehow missed the news of resurrection are walking from Jerusalem to their home in Emmaus when Jesus catches up and, unrecognised, falls into step beside them. He walks the entire journey with them, not revealing his identity but helping them make sense of the events they remember. As they reach their home, he prepares to say goodbye but they press him to stay with them. As they begin their evening meal, the stranger takes and breaks bread – a deeply symbolic action in the Christian community – and, the narrative tells us, they instantly recognise him (even though they have not actually heard about his resurrection). Before they can react, he disappears, and they immediately hurry back to Jerusalem where they join in the jubilation of the rest of the group.

The two friends of Jesus have done what is natural following a traumatic experience – they have removed themselves from the place associated with the pain. The stranger who catches up with them on the road clearly knows that the place where they really need to be – the place where the healing will be found – is the city they have left, and they are walking in entirely the wrong direction; but rather than turn them around, he shares their journey with them. On arrival at their home, he does not presume an invitation – which would allow the conversation to continue – but enters only when they press him to do so. And it is in the familiar ritual action of breaking bread as, characteristically, he serves them (as a guest, he might surely expect to be waited upon rather than to serve), that the awareness dawns. And at the moment of recognition – the moment when it would be most natural for him to stay with them and share in the celebration or even become the object of worship – he disappears!

For a theologian there is a clear message here that the risen Christ is not to be possessed by particular groups or individuals. For the pastoral companion the image says other things about a way of being with people in distress by which the companion doesn't strive to change the direction of their journey but joins them on it, participates in the conversation and simply, by that way of being, allows the hope to emerge before exiting the scene, leaving them freely to decide on their next action.

The two disciples then are shown hurrying back the seven miles or so (presumably on foot and with full stomachs!) to be in the very place that they had been so anxious to leave only hours before.

This story holds particular significance for my wife and myself following a personal bereavement that befell us many years ago (before I had considered becoming a minister). A friend of a family member, hearing about it, offered his home to us as a refuge. He had recently become vicar of a parish many miles away, with a (typical of those times) large, rambling vicarage where he said we were welcome to lose ourselves for a while, joining with him and his family as and when we wished.

So we left, for a while, the place associated with so much pain. The pain naturally came with us, but there was still a sense of refuge from the people, places and activities that intensified it. We knew, of course, that we should have to return to all that, but the respite was welcome and therapeutic.

On our return home, we readied ourselves for the year-long journey of 'firsts' – the activities that would remind us of the huge loss we had suffered and emphasise the gap in our lives. The break had been invaluable in helping us prepare for it, and now the reality had to be faced. One of these was a return to the local church congregation of which we were part. As it was just after Easter, the set reading for the day was this passage we have just been considering. In the sermon, the visiting minister spoke of the need to get away after a traumatic experience; the need that people might feel to remove themselves from the place of pain and take refuge in a different environment – a journey that might be geographical – as it had been for us – psychological or spiritual. We were given an image, from this narrative, of the risen Christ making the journey with us and then enabling us, having found hope in that other place, to return to the place of pain and find hope and a new beginning there.[45]

It was not, of course, a direct parallel. For us, there had been and would be no vision of the person we had lost, but there had been a sense of resurrection faith in terms of our own emotional state at the time: *'This is not the last word: it does not need to be this way.'* Nothing was going to bring back the one we had lost (a fantasy that had in fact been part of the grieving process and would remain so for a while), but something about the people we had been with and the

---

45 This was not a tailored sermon – the minister did not know us, our circumstances or that we would be there but was offering the congregation his pastoral interpretation of the Bible passage set for that day.

healing quality of their presence with us (most of which was utterly unconscious on their part) had enabled us to return to a place where we had hardly thought we might be able to live, in the hope that there might be healing for us there. The sermon that Sunday did not take away the pain or provide any kind of quick fix. But it did raise a banner on our emotional horizon, some long distance ahead, but still clearly readable:

'This is not the last word: it does not need to be this way.'

We have spent some time considering the relevance of Christian spirituality to the task of being a pastoral companion. Some of this may have value when shared with the person whose companion we are. All of it, I believe, has value for us as companions in illustrating and illuminating the process of which we are a part.

We are now ready to consider a topic on which many readers may well be thinking I have been surprisingly silent.

Incarnation, prayer and the pastoral companion

The question of how – and indeed whether – to introduce and conduct prayer as part of a pastoral encounter is one that troubles many companions and, when the question is raised, reveals sharply differing views. I have left the subject until now because I wanted to consider it against the background of *incarnational* faith.

Throughout this part of the book I have been attempting to show how the Christian belief in the Incarnation both challenges and enables us to find the presence of God in humanity. I hope I have shown that this is very far from a simple matter whereby a kind and well-blessed companion reveals divine love to a distressed other – a concept that I find deeply patronising. By contrast, I have cited numerous examples where the revelation has been in the opposite direction – where as a companion I have had the unspeakable privilege of seeing what Irenaeus called 'the glory of God [in] humanity fully alive' vividly manifest through the medium of the other. So there is no simple division here, and it cannot be emphasised strongly enough that neither party is exclusively either the active mediator or the passive recipient of that experience. Belief in Incarnation means that the active presence of God (whether recognised or not) is a given in any human encounter – and it is through the *process* that the revelation occurs. That concept is fundamental to my understanding of 'prayer'.

If we accept the basic premise I have presented, and if we think of prayer as being an act of relating with God, then the entire encounter between companion and other is prayer – not just 'as good as' or even 'a kind of', but simply and unequivocally prayer. Indeed, as we have seen, it is a particularly powerful form of prayer in which a positively awesome encounter between human and divine – and the amazing relationship between those two – is manifest in ways that for me are unsurpassed by any other experience. Of course, I would not suggest that it is the only form of prayer – as with our day-to-day relationships with one another, there are many other ways to communicate – but we should not underestimate the value of the encounter as not simply equal to but in many cases the best possible form of prayer.

I well remember a listening exercise undertaken during my ministerial training in which we were asked to spend time together in small groups, speaking and hearing about whatever concerns any might wish to share, and to pray together. It so happened that one member of the group, whom I shall call Harry, was deeply troubled about something in particular, and the group willingly allowed that to occupy the entire session. As the time went on, however, one student became increasingly agitated and repeatedly interrupted, saying, 'We must stop or we shan't have time to pray!' The consensus of the group, though (including Harry), was that what we were doing *was* prayer, and not only prayer but the best and most appropriate form of it for that moment. We had recognised his particular need to be heard and it would have been pastorally insensitive to guillotine that listening in favour of a formalised 'prayer', effectively bypassing him in order to satisfy our own need to think we had 'talked to God'.

I find it very difficult to believe that the God present during that conversation needed further direct requests or instructions from any of us. Any member of the group who might have had the power to assist our colleague would surely have been moved to do so and, to be candid, it seems to me offensive to believe that a God of infinite love and compassion would need any further prompting from the student group. It would, of course, have been wrong to impose that view on 'Harry' – which is why he was asked. Had he replied that he would value some time spent in conventional prayer then naturally that would have been respected.

There are many times when prayer in its more generally understood form is appropriate to meet the needs of the other. We should not underestimate the immense value to many people of hearing themselves included in – or made the specific topic of – prayer. There may be many reasons for this, perhaps connected with the status they perceive that the companion has or perhaps their own lack of confidence in framing the words. It can also be a good form of the 'summarising' we considered earlier as one of the listening skills. For all kinds of reasons, it might well be that formalised prayer is absolutely appropriate – whereas in other situations it might be preferable to avoid it. Because of the beliefs I have already expressed, I have to confess that when a companion offers to pray with or for me as 'other' in that kind of way I tend to decline politely, explaining that I have had the experience of being truly and deeply heard and understood by a companion and, for me (and I emphasise 'for me'), anything else is superfluous and likely to be an anticlimax.

What this says is that it is important that the use of prayer arises from the relationship between companion and other. We should not be adopting, in this of all areas, a 'one size fits all' approach. It is important to be very aware of the other's needs before simply indulging in a formulaic prayer – or indeed, not doing so.

This brings me to a particular concern I have in this area: what are the expectations of the other in terms of the outcome of the prayer? And following on from that, how will we respond to their disappointment if those hopes are not met? I remember a church worshipper I used to visit at home who was experiencing great hostility from his neighbours and who wanted me to say a 'prayer of protection'. When I asked what he hoped the outcome would be, he was crystal clear: I was to ask God very specifically to stop the harassment and ensure that no harm came to him. And that would be that. There were, of course, innumerable texts he was able to cite from Scripture to support his confident belief that this would happen.

I was concerned to understand more about the situation. *Why* did he feel persecuted by his neighbours? There were many possibilities, both subjective and objective, interior and exterior, and I did not share his confidence that what for me amounted to an attempted quick fix – a magic spell masquerading as an act of faith – was going to resolve any of it. I did believe, though, that *incarnate* God already was intimately involved, living, suffering, dying, rising, protesting within the no-doubt complex matrix of personal and social issues, and was deeply and passionately concerned for the healing and wholeness of all involved.

This is where some of the things we have looked at earlier come back into play. We need to listen very deeply to 'the question behind the question' (see chapter 2) – the concerns and factors that underlie what my pastoral tutors used to call 'the presenting issue' (as distinct from the substantive need). On the basis of that listening, we may decide to say a carefully phrased prayer or to engage more deeply and widely with the real issues. Perhaps we might suggest that the other speak to their GP about anxiety management groups, or we may feel that there is an issue for referral (with the other's permission) to a community group, social services or other appropriate agency. There is, of course, no reason why all of that process cannot also involve traditional forms of prayer which the other might find supportive and encouraging – but we are thinking about prayer, not quick fixes.

So for me the question of prayer needs to be approached in the same way as any other issue that arises, and considered carefully with the other's well-being at the centre of our awareness. Like any other aspect of pastoral companionship, it is not to be used in doctrinaire or formulaic ways but always with acute consciousness of its place in the wider activity of companionship.

Over the book as a whole, I have tried to communicate not only the healing power of presence – of our simply being there with another – but also the personal fulfilment and joy that it can bring. I have also indicated, I hope, that the position of pastoral companion is one of serious responsibility and which needs to be undertaken with awareness of the very real dangers, both for the companion and the other.

So it is that we come to the essential final chapter where we shall consider the matters of good practice, ethics and safeguards essential to the provision of the service. These are especially applicable where formal arrangements are being put in place, such as in churches and other organisations providing pastoral companionship as part of their service to their members or to the community.

10

Good practice, ethics and safeguards

The positioning of this chapter at the end of the book should not be taken as a reflection of its importance, as if it were an incidental footnote or afterthought. It actually addresses matters of the highest priority. Indeed, I originally placed it at the beginning but moved it because I felt it more helpful to begin opening up the main subject matter as quickly as possible and that this topic might be easier to relate to after that.

Having said that, it can, of course, be argued that wherever it is positioned, a chapter is never going to cover the subject. When it comes to matters of ethics, good practice and safeguards for the companion and the carer, there are organisations whose specific function it is to advise on those and to provide resources for companions as well as for team leaders and supervisors.

My approach here, then, will be to do two things. Firstly, I will say a few words about the importance of these matters and highlight some issues that are of particular significance in the pastoral care field. Secondly, I will seek to provide some information about where to find authoritative guidance along with resources and ongoing support.

I would strongly advocate three things as a minimum basis for offering pastoral companionship:

Firstly, any person involved in the provision of pastoral companionship to another should earnestly consider some form of membership with an appropriate national body. This may be individual membership or inclusion in the church's organisational membership referred to below. Some of these national bodies are listed at the end of this chapter. Companions who are qualified as counsellors or psychotherapists will certainly know, and almost certainly already be members, of one of the two professional bodies – BACP or UKCP.

Secondly, any church, faith community or other organisation having or seeking to develop a designated pastoral team, irrespective of team members' individual affiliations, should at the very least adopt a clear good-practice framework within which all pastoral companions in that setting work. For Christian churches, the framework of Pastoral Care UK (as part of ACC) will probably be appropriate – or at least a good model from which to begin, adapting it to specific circumstances where necessary. Similar examples (and with them other related resources) may well be available from denominational central offices, but as I write, this is not universally the case.

Thirdly, any church, faith community or other organisation having or seeking to develop a designated pastoral team, irrespective of team members' individual affiliations, should seriously consider organisational membership of one of the national associations. This will provide a number of benefits, including:

- Objective, widely recognised standards and criteria.
- Awareness of important issues that may not be immediately obvious to the church leadership team.
- Regular information about developments in legislation and convention that affect the provision of the service and the care of those affected as companions or others.
- A sense of belonging and support for members of the team.
- A firm reference point for beginning to consider difficult issues that might arise during the work, whether for pastoral companions or the organisers/supervisors.
- Readily available, quality training and information on difficult subjects such as supervision and confidentiality.
- Assurance to the church's insurers that the pastoral care is being offered and practised responsibly as a starting point for defence against possible allegations or claims for damages.

Many of the matters that I should otherwise have felt obliged to deal with will be more effectively addressed through consultation with and/or membership of those national bodies. Clearly, working in that way should not be seen as an alternative to the particular denomination's own training and support facilities, but is likely to supplement and complement them in important ways.

As I write this, I have to say that my research among the churches has suggested that what is offered is often patchy and by no means comprehensive. This is unfortunate, because there are some aspects of good practice that I think are more difficult for pastoral companions than for counsellors, and the clear principles that apply in clinical environments are much more difficult to adhere to strictly. Let's consider a few examples of those.

Parameters and expectations

In a clinical setting, roles are very clearly defined: my work with this person takes place within a specific context with its own disciplines, expectations and parameters. It is also very likely that I am not the only professional from my organisation but am part of a multidisciplinary team. This helps greatly because I can often manage the parameters by simply saying something like, 'Well, that's outside my area – maybe you should speak with your social worker about that.' A pastoral companion could make a similar response but will often be less confident to do so; they will not be directly relating to the social worker, even if they can be sure there is one. So it is very easy to find oneself being drawn into conversations that are outside our area of competence. The other, however, might not fully realise this, as they regard the companion as someone to be trusted, and may well take unwise actions based upon what is said.

With this in mind, it is very important that anyone involved in the provision of pastoral care is clear about the extent of responsibilities and is enabled to resist the pressure or temptation to work beyond them.

Knowing our place

The term 'pastoral care' is delightfully and worryingly open ended. It's great to be open to the needs of the other without the necessary but sometimes awkward restrictions that closer definition might bring, but it can be also lead to uncertainty, misunderstandings and resentment – or even to a companion getting in over their head. For example, for a young and fit companion it might be quite reasonable to go up a set of steps and change a light bulb if requested by an infirm person, whereas an older or less confident companion would probably be well advised to decline and to pass on the request to someone more suited to the task.

In my last pastorate, we were fortunate to have a retired man who in his seventies could outwalk, outcycle and generally outdo many men half his age, and he also had extensive building and DIY skills. He was willing and well able to be called upon for all manner of tasks – including going up scaffolding and fixing roofs! Such versatility in one person is unusual, and it is important for every member of a pastoral team to be aware of willing *and competent* volunteers who are available – and be ready to call upon them when appropriate.

Another way of getting in over our heads is illustrated by an embarrassing incident that occurred during my early days of informal pastoral work. I still wince as I remember the ferocity of the attack launched upon me by an understandably angry fellow worshipper who told me in no uncertain terms that I was *not* to describe her to her elderly mother as an interfering busybody who was talking nonsense. I had, in fact, said nothing of the sort, but had apparently been led into appearing to agree (no doubt for the sake of politeness in the moment) with the elder lady's assessment of it. I can't remember the exact topic of conversation now, but it's quite possible that the mother's comment to me about her daughter had been quite restrained but later, in the heat of a family argument, been expressed much more forcefully and with my alleged endorsement. I quickly learnt to field such remarks in neutral ways or, more appropriately, with an empathic response focusing on the person's feelings rather than their opinions.

It's impossible in any text book, let alone a paragraph in a chapter of this work, to give comprehensive advice, but generally knowing our role and our limitations – and adhering to them – is a good principle.

Caring for ourselves

There is something about the general perception of omnicompetence and a (sometimes frankly unrealistic) concept of sacrificial self-giving that can easily seduce us into making ourselves indispensable. For a while it may well feel good – or at least flattering – until the reality that we are nothing of the sort catches up with us. It is difficult, of course, for perfectly laudable reasons, to decline to help when that is appropriate, but all the counsellors' and carers' professional bodies, in my experience, make caring for our own well-being an ethical requirement. We should not be offering care to another when we are physically or emotionally drained, so avoiding that state of affairs is part of our responsibility. Far from being selfish, part of our good, responsible care for the other is that we also care for ourselves.

I well remember assuring an elderly gentleman in a congregation that I would always be available to him and he should never be afraid to call me. He wasn't – especially when he realised after an enjoyable and extended evening out that he was not really fit to drive home and preferred not to 'waste money paying for a taxi'. This might, of course, have been a reasonable request to make to a friend or relative, but when made to someone with pastoral responsibility for a large number of people, it took on a different character altogether. I found it terribly difficult to know how to handle: I was new both to ministry and to that church and didn't want to appear unwilling – but clearly there needed to be a shared understanding of what I was there to do.

Giving the easy answer at the time – 'Yes, of course' – turned out not to be a good precedent to set, and I was neither the first nor sadly the last minister to have found myself in the situation of running myself ragged being nice to people in ways that were not my responsibility and then being too physically, mentally or emotionally exhausted to do the things that were. So managing expectations – something we considered when reflecting on the Exodus tradition – is an important aspect of staying within safe parameters.

Opinions, advice and information

I have mentioned the general misconception of counselling and pastoral care as involving the giving of sage advice. This again is difficult for pastoral companions as we do not always have the option of referring to an appropriate expert, and we certainly do not want to rebuff people with whom we share both friendship and the pews (a point we shall consider further shortly). Something that might be helpful is to clarify the necessary distinctions between opinion, advice and information. The last, if we are confident we have or can find it, may well be within our remit, whereas the other two are quite another matter.

If someone were to ask about the best way to get to the next town, there might be a number of possible responses:

- 'Well, there's always the bus – but I hate buses: all those people crammed together with their coughs and splutters. I never travel on them, myself.'

This clearly falls into the category of opinion – and a particularly uninformed and probably prejudiced one at that. While it might be expressed among friends at a dinner party, it is not appropriate for a pastoral companionship context.

- 'Oh, if I were you I'd go by rail. There's normally plenty of space on the 10.15, but do make sure you sit in the middle carriage so that if there's a collision you're in the best part of the train.'

This is direct advice, prescribing a course of action, offered on the basis of subjective preference and opinion. Is there any research basis to show that the middle carriage is safer (the logic may seem obvious, but that is not necessarily any guide)? Even if correct in itself, the recommendation does not take into account any of the particular needs of the other – who might, for example, wish to visit a particular store which is close to the bus station and a mile from the rail terminus! In addition to that, I prefer not to imagine the feelings of this companion were the other then to be on the train when an accident occurred in which only the occupants of the central carriage were harmed.

- 'Well, there's a bus stop outside the Rose and Crown and there's a regular train service – the station's about ten minutes' walk away – and there's also a taxi rank round the corner on East Street. That's about as much as I know I'm afraid, but if you'd like me to help you search online for more information . . .'

The companion has responded in a helpful way with what information she knows, leaving the decision to the other. She has admitted the limitations of her own knowledge and offered some practical help in an area where she feels confident to do so. This goes beyond a counsellor's remit but may well be appropriate for the much broader role of a pastoral companion who has the necessary knowledge and skills.

These are just a few examples of the importance of knowing our own limits and those of our role – something that should receive better coverage in training, supervision and in the documentation covering a pastoral team.

Wider relationships

I referred earlier to the fact that a counsellor in a clinical practice would be unlikely to know the family and friends of a client other than through what the client were to say – leaving aside any chance encounters in the waiting room – and the professional boundaries are very clear in that the relationship is strictly with the client who is only seen in that setting. However, in a faith community context, things could hardly be expected to be that simple. The person to whom we are companion is probably part of a congregation or social circle that includes us and many others known to us both, and this can bring its own difficulties. Similarly, we may encounter each other at church coffee mornings, in services of worship and in many other settings.

This can create particular sensitivities for a pastoral companion which will be different, but still potentially present, according to whether the companion's relationship with the other is generally known. We shall doubtless be involved in general chit-chat at times when the name of the other might arise quite innocently. Someone mentions that 'Tom' does not seem quite well at the moment, and understandable speculation begins about the cause. It is very tempting to become involved in such conversations, perhaps with the well-intentioned aim of stopping inaccurate rumours from circulating. But the trouble is that as soon as we let it be known that we have special knowledge, we begin to get drawn into a dangerous area where everything we say is open to similarly wayward speculation, and we may unwittingly fuel that. If the ensuing rumours reach the ears of the other concerned – with the companion's name attached – the pastoral relationship may be seriously threatened. And even if it doesn't, the mere prospect of it can cast a shadow from the companion's side.

On the other hand, the pastoral relationship may be well known – it is often common knowledge that certain individuals are regular visitors for particular members – and the assumption that we have some esoteric knowledge will create expectations by others involved in the conversation. At such times we need to stay firmly on the sidelines, or further, and be ready to field any leading questions with non-committal responses. A couple that are quite useful are, 'I really couldn't say,' or 'There's nothing I can really add to what you say.' This, being quite true as far as it goes, may hopefully be sufficient.

What must be controlled at all times – understandable though it certainly is – is the temptation to hint that we know something. It is not unnatural to feel a sense of pride that someone has chosen us to be the holders of sensitive or deeply personal information. Evidently they trust us, feel at ease with us, and so on – and that is always flattering. It may seem harmless to drop a hint that we have been given that position, but again it will almost certainly lead us into dangerous waters where almost anything we say – including nothing – will be interpreted, and not necessarily to anyone's good.

It may at times be necessary simply to avoid contact with social huddles where such conversations are in progress, or where they might become so, and we need to develop sensitive antennae allied to a generally discreet manner.

This leads us to perhaps the most vital consideration of all.

Confidentiality

Undoubtedly, a particularly serious concern for any pastoral team (which we touched upon in chapter 2, 'Qualities of presence') must be the issue of confidentiality and what it means in that context which, again, is different from the professional situation in ways that can be difficult. But let's begin by defining what we mean by confidentiality.

'Can you keep a secret?'

General understandings – or rather misunderstandings – of confidentiality range from dark secrecy that can be interpreted as furtive to 'Only to be disclosed to people I trust'. Sadly, since everyone has someone they feel they can trust – especially when some juicy titbit of information is just bursting to escape – that definition means that everybody soon knows about it (or a version of it).

The International Charter defines confidentiality as 'ensuring that information is accessible only to those authorized to have access and is protected throughout its lifecycle.'[46]

This is much better. Confidentiality is about the *appropriate management* of information so that those who genuinely need to know – and are appropriately authorised – have access to it, but others are denied. This is not the same thing as either complete secrecy or telling the people we choose to, or whom we trust.

It is not uncommon for church officers and other senior lay leaders – for understandable reasons – to feel they have a need and indeed a right to know about the pastoral needs of others. This is understandable. In my own denomination, elders are conscious that there is a pastoral element to their role and may well consider that not being told about someone's marriage difficulties, for example, compromises that. Sometimes, they may take the minister's or pastoral companion's discretion as a sign that they are not trusted, which is not the issue.

The real question is about who rightly owns the information and has the right to decide who else should have it. The defining issue for me as a minister was not, 'Do I trust you enough to tell you this?' (that might well come later) but rather, 'Does the person whose information this is want you to know it?' and if not, 'Is there a compelling reason why you need to know it, nonetheless?'[47] The person whose information it rightly is may, of course, choose for themselves to disclose it to people whom they trust, and that is their right and their risk. The fact that they have done so, even after asking us to hold it secure, does not in any way loosen the bond of confidentiality.

So the vital difference between confidentiality and secrecy lies in the phrase, 'accessible only to those authorized to have access'. Sometimes there are legal or policy requirements governing this, and our role is to ensure that those to whom we are companions are aware of those. The most obvious examples would concern the abuse

---

46 International Charter Confidentiality Policy. Available at www.internationalcharter. org/confidentiality.html (accessed 12 March 2015).
47 The latter question would usually be about the possibility of serious harm to someone.

of people when they are vulnerable. Abuse might be, for example, emotional, financial, physical or sexual, and 'people when they are vulnerable' might include (among others) children, the elderly, the infirm, people with mental impairments and learning difficulties or indeed anyone at particular times and circumstances. This area is covered by legislation, and pastoral team convenors should be aware of the information and ensure that it is covered in training and supervision.

When (fortunately rarely or even never for most pastoral companions) the need to break confidentiality arises, the issue of trust comes to the fore and it needs to be handled well. The other must be the first to know that this is to happen; they must be given a clear explanation of both the reasons and the general range of information to be imparted, and a written note must be made of the conversation as soon afterwards as is practicable. In all this and in all that follows it must never be forgotten that the situation arose because the other trusted the companion – a trust that remains a privilege and an honour even when disclosure has to be made for good reason.

Record keeping

The mention of a written note above raises this difficult question. It is one that can always be guaranteed to start animated debates among counsellors, and probably even more so among pastoral companions. It is easy to see that the person who enjoys a visit from a pastoral companion – a visit characterised mainly by conversation and caffeine – might at the very least raise an eyebrow at the idea that notes would later be made about the meeting – and the companion likewise at the prospect of a generous offer of time and commitment resulting in their being swept away on a dreaded avalanche of paperwork! Clearly, this would be inappropriate and unhelpful to both parties, to say the least. On the other hand, some conversations (such as we have just considered) demand to be recorded, as much for the companion's as the other's well-being. The main thing I would say is that this is one of those issues that needs to be a matter of local policy, bearing in mind relevant legislation, and in policy terms will probably be a case for flexible guidelines rather than rigid rules.

The elephant is now in the room, though, and the question that must be addressed is about the content and custody of any notes that do have to be made.[48] If notes are handwritten, where are they

---

48 This whole area is, of course, the subject of Data Protection legislation, binding on all citizens and which should be part of the knowledge base of team administrators.

kept? Ideally the church office would include a locked cabinet,[49] but in many cases they are likely to be kept in the companion's home, at least when they are first written. Essentially, they should be in a part of the house where children do not play, where visitors would not be expected to go, and where they can be discreetly accommodated if not actually locked away. In the case of computer notes, things are very different.

On the face of it, a password-protected computer might seem more secure than a desk drawer, but there is a serious problem. Doubtless, if it is a personal computer, it will some day be replaced or disposed of, and what will then become of it? Perhaps it will be given to a friend, or sold on eBay – and it is well known that completely erasing data from a hard drive is notoriously difficult. The pastoral companion may feel that the computer is safe, but a curious and technically talented person[50] might quickly recover the 'deleted' files from deep in the system. Any computer used in the course of pastoral work should be made safe before disposal by the removal and safe storage – or preferably destruction – of the hard disk – which is where, if anywhere, the information should be, and not 'in the cloud'.

It would probably be unrealistic to expect companions not to use a personal computer at all, but what should be very carefully avoided is the recording in insecure ways of what we used to call PID – personally identifiable data. This would obviously include names and addresses, but it does not stop there. There could be other details – possibly about a person's role in a church fellowship, their work, hobbies or other matters that would make their identity obvious to anyone who knows them. All these and similar details would come under the heading of PID. A little imaginative phrasing and sometimes the use of clues known only to the pastoral companion can usually get around this, but the issue does need to be high in the awareness of anyone who feels they need to make a record of a pastoral conversation.

Once notes are made, another tricky issue arises around the right to access them – for the other and also, for example, for statutory authorities. Notes can be demanded by a court hearing a case where the other is either a complainant or defendant – and in either case will probably be used by one side or the other in ways not liked by the person concerned. This is another reason for being sparing in the keeping of notes and careful about the nature of the information or comments – especially comments – they contain.

---

49 This still might not meet the need: how many people have access to it?
50 I am not the only person to have observed that the best person to ask for help with computers is generally the nearest teenager!

The right of access by the person who is the subject of them should be taken as read, and this clearly affects the nature of the notes themselves. This whole area is one that needs to be explored with either denominational or secular organisations that have relevant expertise. Legislation covering data protection is notoriously changeable, and up-to-date information must be sought from the appropriate authorities. This same observation is equally true in terms of the next topic.

Safeguarding

This is the term used for the process of ensuring that children and vulnerable adults are protected from the danger of abuse by people in positions of relative power – whether the abuse be physical, emotional, financial, sexual, etc. It has been alluded to briefly above in considering the need to share confidential information where that is a concern. However, the responsibility for safeguarding begins long before that stage and must be considered in the appointment of pastoral companions who will in all probability be spending time in the homes of people who are vulnerable to one or more forms of abuse.

This is no longer a matter for debate in the church: it is a legal requirement, and the consequences of neglect can be severe. The exact provisions of the law are complex and have a way of changing subtly from time to time. The responsibility is upon the local church's governing body to ensure that the provision of pastoral companionship complies with all the current legislation at any given time.

For this purpose, enquiries should be made of the denominational authorities who should have a member of staff whose designated area of responsibility this is and who will advise upon the checks that need to be carried out and the precautions that should be put in place. It is to be hoped that all churches have already formulated and adopted policies for safeguarding, and implemented their provisions, which should cover the bases also for pastoral companions. However, even if that is the case, it is a wise (and indeed responsible) approach not only to take advice early on but also to put measures in place to ensure that the provisions are reviewed and updated regularly.

I have been saddened sometimes to find this regarded within churches as a tiresome imposition of red tape. Surely, safeguarding the well-being of people when they are vulnerable is something that should be a top priority. If anything, we should welcome the provision of a proper framework that makes clear what is expected of us so that we can know with confidence that we are doing what is necessary. Think what we would give for that kind of clarity in other areas of our lives!

By way of an illustration, I recall being on a routine visit to the home of a church member who lived alone when she suddenly became ill and required hospitalisation. Having called the ambulance and done what I could, I unexpectedly found myself the custodian of her keys – and therefore all her worldly possessions and personal information – with instructions to lock up the house and keep the keys safe until her return. That kind of occurrence is rare, but nonetheless it is always a possibility for any pastoral companion – and such a position of trust places responsibilities on the church.

Supervision[51] and support

This again is too large a subject to be treated adequately here, and I shall circumvent most of it by noting that excellent information, advice, training and ongoing support is available from the national organisations listed at the end of the chapter. However, there are some specific matters affecting the church setting that it is important to highlight even though, again, I am not necessarily able to offer solutions and which must be addressed by those whose fields of expertise and responsibility they are.

I am hoping (I see some encouraging signs but not as many as I might like) that things have moved on from the situation a number of years ago when, at a ministers' conference for a particular denomination, I raised (from the floor) the subject of supervision for ordained ministers in pastorates. The general response of the assembled clergy was sceptical – even, from some of them, scornful – and the senior denominational officer leading the session dismissed the whole subject with the dusty response, 'If ministers feel the need for supervision they can go out and get it!' Apart from the question of whether it should be left to the subjective awareness of individual ministers, the statement was lamentably untrue: most ministers at that time would have had great difficulty even beginning the search in an informed way, and even if they were able, there would have been little for them to find.

Hopefully, as I say, we have moved on from that. It should now be taken for granted that anyone working with others who may be

---

51 It is worth repeating at this point that supervision in this context is not about management or about 'Big Brother' but the appropriate support of pastoral companions and their work.

vulnerable needs supervision. At the very least, from time to time, as companions on others' journeys, we shall ourselves have the need for someone to enable us to reflect on our work and its effect upon our own well-being – or indeed to help us to disentangle complex issues or handle a delicate situation.

What is supervision?

The word 'supervision' would seem to imply that someone is sitting in on the meeting between the companion and the other, but this is certainly not the case. The supervisor would see the companion quite separately. 'Supervision' means 'oversight' and really refers to someone viewing the work from a different vantage point – someone who, not being directly involved in the day-to-day companionship, may see a broader picture, and also see the companion objectively. In formal counselling, this is an important part of the supervisor's role: to be aware of the well-being of the counsellor who might be in danger of losing sight of that because their attention is so focused on the other. The supervisor will also, however, generally bring greater experience and training to the role and will be able to highlight aspects of the work – including dangers and opportunities – that might otherwise be missed.

This is good and right, but in a faith community setting there are serious difficulties that need to be addressed by those in leadership when any pastoral care provision is being set up.

Too much information

In a clinical setting, individual supervision takes place in private, between the supervisor and the therapist, and the discussion is about cases, not named people – so the supervisor will generally not know the name of the client. Clients are always informed as part of the contracting process that the work will be discussed in this way, and any other factors affecting confidentiality will be understood and agreed.

Within a faith community or similar setting, this becomes more difficult. The obvious person to provide supervision might seem to be the minister or whoever has overall pastoral charge. The difficulty regarding confidentiality immediately becomes clear: a supervisor in a clinical setting is unlikely to recognise the client from the therapist's description of the work, but that is certainly not true in a faith community where a minister who knows the congregation well will doubtless quickly identify others from what their pastoral companions say. This will then become an issue not only of confidentiality but also of dual relationships concerning the minister or supervisor and the other.

The obvious answer to this is to find supervision outside the immediate church setting but within the wider church, and here the denominational officers will have an important role to play in setting up the necessary systems, providing training and support for supervisors, etc. This would generally imitate the pattern followed in the clinical world. My clinical supervision was provided by a clinical psychologist who worked in a very different area of the Trust but came under the same general policies and procedures. Had we found that she knew one of my clients personally, we should have sought another supervisor for that particular case.

That was relatively straightforward in that setting, but is less simple in the churches. Most congregations will include people who are known to members of other congregations. Some will sit on committees that are part of the wider councils of the church and some may have a role there that involves their visiting other churches in the area, knowing and being known to a great number of people. It's easy to see, then, that finding an appropriately qualified and experienced supervisor for pastoral companions may be somewhat less straightforward than it sounds – which may be one reason why raising the subject has not always met with a favourable response. However, the fact that something is difficult does not mean it should not be done, and it is important that the matter is addressed. The expertise and experience is all out there – what we need in the churches is the will to access it.

Onward referrals

I remember a conversation with a primary school head, many years ago, concerning a child who was clearly struggling to cope in the educational environment, and for whom some kind of specialised provision was being considered as a temporary measure to enable the difficulties to be addressed so that the pupil could later be returned to the school to continue in mainstream education. The head's response was not encouraging: 'In all my career I've never had to refer a child to another service and I'm not going to start now.' Thankfully, the local authority overruled and the child was transferred to a very particular kind of unit, still within mainstream education but equipped and skilled to address his specific needs.

It was an inexpressible joy to watch the child blossom in the new situation and – in a remarkably short space of time – come to love learning and eagerly look forward to each day at school (and to the return to his previous class).

Some of the cases I have mentioned in the course of this book have been of a similar nature, where it would be natural for the pastoral companion to feel that the best way to help the person would be to refer them, with the person's knowledge and permission, to a more specialised service such as, for example, Cruse or the Compassionate Friends. It might in some cases be appropriate even to suggest they consult their General Practitioner about clinical services available through that channel. In an organised pastoral team, part of the role of the coordinator is to have information to hand about a range of agencies and referral routes. It is clearly impossible to give a list of those here, but information is readily available through GP surgeries, social services departments, child-welfare and bereavement charities and so on, and will, of course, include services peculiar to the locality.

It is important when considering onward referral that it is clearly understood by both companion and other to be about responsible caring and not about either of them 'giving up' on the person or process they are with. The suggestion might come from either, and while it is natural for the companion to feel a twinge of hurt pride, that should be congruently recognised for what it is. Similarly, the companion will want to do everything possible to avoid a sense of rejection on the part of the other.

In the case of an official pastoral care team, an agreed process for onward referral should be part of the operational policy, but the exact details will vary according to circumstances. In a church or faith community setting, it will inevitably be the case that the two people will continue to be in contact, if only over coffee after worship. The companion, while no doubt continuing to be interested in the well-being of the other, will certainly need to take care not to intrude upon the new process of which she or he is no longer a part. We are back to the issue about letting go, discussed when reflecting upon Exodus.

Any possibility of onward referral is something that should be considered in supervision, whether that be formal supervision or a quiet chat with the minister or pastoral team leader (with the permission of the other), and the conversation should include not only the needs of the other but the feelings of the companion, too.

Sources of support for churches and pastors

As I reach the end of the book I do not feel inclined to call it a 'conclusion'. There are a great many loose ends dangling – sometimes tantalisingly so as I have raised awareness of issues to which I cannot provide simple answers. So this is where I 'practise what I preach' and refer the reader on to other sources of help.

It must by now be clear, but bears repetition, that none of the subjects in this book has been covered comprehensively – by a country mile! To do so would be beyond the scope of any one book and certainly of any one writer, however vast their knowledge and experience. So my approach here will be to signpost a few sources of information, support and resources that we might confidently expect to keep themselves up to date in months and years to come.

As suggested earlier, churches seeking support for their provision of pastoral companionship would be best advised first of all to approach the appropriate people in their own denominational councils, whether that be diocese, circuit, synod, association or whatever. Independent churches may be affiliated to bodies such as the Evangelical Alliance or to the Federation of Independent Evangelical Churches. That is the place to begin.

However fruitful those enquiries may be, we have already seen the benefits that might come from being affiliated to an independent, reputable, national organisation specifically concerned with counselling and pastoral care, and I would certainly urge, again, that this be given very serious consideration.

I list below the bodies most likely to be able to offer support in this area. The list is not intended to be exhaustive, but should at least be a good starting point for most churches and Christian organisations.[52]

British Association for Counselling and Psychotherapy (BACP)

www.bacp.co.uk

The national professional body for counselling and psychotherapy, BACP has a spirituality and pastoral care section (BACP Spirituality – http://bacpspirituality.org.uk) that appropriately qualified ministers

---

52 All web addresses have been checked and are correct at time of writing.

and pastoral workers may find helpful to join. BACP has an ethical framework to which all members are required to adhere, and issues further statements of ethical practice from time to time. These together might form a useful model for other organisations seeking to develop something tailored to their specific needs.

United Kingdom Council for Psychotherapy (UKCP)

www.psychotherapy.org.uk

This organisation, with very strict membership criteria, is only accessible to pastoral companions if they are training or already qualified as psychotherapists. Like BACP, it is a highly respected professional body and is acknowledged here as a matter of respect.

Association of Christian Counsellors (ACC)

http://www.acc-uk.org/

This organisation seeks to offer and support high-quality counselling informed by Christian faith and spirituality. It also includes a specific membership section for people involved in pastoral care and publishes guidelines for good practice which would be useful for churches either to adopt outright or to use as a model. In addition, a wide range of training, education and support is on offer.

Pastoral Care UK (as part of ACC)

This is the name of ACC's specific division for pastoral care which has its own dedicated website at: www.pastoralcareuk.org

Institute of Pastoral Counselling (IPC)

www.pastoral-counselling.co.uk

IPC is a body exploring connections between the psychological sciences, theology and pastoral care that ministers, team leaders and companions may find a valuable source of information and training.

Cruse Bereavement Care

www.cruse.org.uk

Cruse has great experience in offering companionship to people affected by bereavement, and also provides training and placement facilities for bereavement counsellors. It may be an organisation to access either for referral purposes or for expertise and experience.

Winston's Wish

www.winstonswish.org.uk

A charity for offering support for bereaved children and a possible reference point especially where those caring for the children are themselves hindered in doing so by their own grief.

Relate

www.relate.org

The relationship specialist, Relate has a long history of offering support to people in relational difficulties. Formerly the Marriage Guidance Council, it dropped the 'Marriage' tag from its title many years ago and has great experience and insight in many areas of relationships.

Compassionate Friends

www.tcf.org.uk

An organisation specifically offering support to people who have experienced the death of a child.

References

Barrett-Lennard, Godfrey T., *Carl Rogers' Helping System, Journey and Substance* (Sage 1998)

Bonhoeffer, Dietrich, *Letters and Papers from Prison (SCM Press 2001)*

Glasson, Barbara, *Finding a Way* (Kevin Mayhew, 2015)

St Irenaeus (second century Bishop of Lyons), *Against Heresies, Book 4, 20:7 (c185 CE)*

Jung, Carl, *The Practice of Psychotherapy* (Ark Paperbacks)

Kushner, Harold, *When Bad Things Happen to Good People* (Pan, 2002)

Paul McCartney, John Lennon, 'The Fool on the Hill', Copyright © Sony/ATV Tunes LLC

Macquarrie, John, *Principles of Christian Theology* (SCM 1979)

McClelland, Kate, *Call the Chaplain* (Canterbury Press 2014)

Nouwen, Henri J. M., *The Wounded Healer* (Darton, Longman & Todd 1994)

Nouwen, Henri J. M., *The Inner Voice of Love* (Darton, Longman & Todd 2014)

Placher, William C., *Narratives of a Vulnerable God* (Westminster John Knox Press, Louisville, Kentucky, 1994)

Rogers, Carl R., *On Becoming a Person* (Constable 1961, reprinted 2001)

Rogers, Carl R., *Client-Centred Therapy* (Constable 1965, reprinted 2001)

Rogers, Carl R., *The Foundations of the Person-Centred Approach* (1979) http://www.elementsuk.com/libraryofarticles/foundations.pdf (accessed 19 March 2015)

Royal College of Psychiatrists: www.rcpsych.ac.uk/mentalhealthinformation/therapies/spirituality andmentalhealth.aspx

Shakespeare, William, *Twelfth Night*

Wordsworth, William, Ode: Intimations of Immortality (V) from *Recollections of Early Childhood*

Wosket, Val, *The Therapeutic Use of Self* (Routledge 1999) (e-edition 2002)